Naked and Awake

Kaayla Vedder

Manor House

Library and Archives Canada Cataloguing in Publication

Vedder, Kaayla, author
  Naked and awake : break the rules, lose control, and reclaim your life /Kaayla Vedder.

ISBN 978-1-988058-22-1 (softcover).--
ISBN 978-1-988058-23-8 (hardcover)

  1. Self-actualization (Psychology). I. Title.

BF637.S4V42 2017   158.1   C2017-904832-5

Printed and bound in Canada / First Edition.
Front Cover Illustration: Alexander Von Ness
Cover Design-layout / Interior- layout: Michael Davie
Interior edit: Susan Crossman, Crossman
Communications
192 pages. All rights reserved.
Published Sept. 21, 2017
Manor House Publishing Inc.
452 Cottingham Crescent, Ancaster, ON, L9G 3V6
www.manor-house.biz
(905) 648-2193

"This project has been made possible [in part] by the Government of Canada. « *Ce projet a été rendu possible [en partie] grâce au gouvernement du Canada.*"

Funded by the Government of Canada
Financé par le gouvernement du Canada

I dedicate this book to my amazing daughters, Kylee & Cassidy. They are inspirational and loving catalysts for change.

"The most profound shifts happen on the other side of comfortable."

Acknowledgements

I would like to share how grateful I am to the entire Universe, Source, God, for conspiring to bring all of these amazing people into my life, assisting to make my journey so juicy and delicious, even when it was perceptively uncomfortable. They include: the beautiful family I was born into, with all the agreements made from that euphoric place of divine love; my sister, who agreed to be one of my first catalysts for me waking up to who I am, instead of who others wanted me to be, my mom, who always kept an open mind, and continues to support me on my journey; and my sweet father who only ever agreed to know as much as he was comfortable with and simply loved me.

To Bryan, aka Buddha, or Baboo, my sweet loving husband, thank you for supporting me in so many ways, lovingly being my biggest cheerleader. I know it can't always be easy being married to me, however you make it seamless.

To all my kids, biological or not, thank you for simply being open to new experiences.

To my two miracles, Kylee and Cassidy, thank you for choosing me to be your mom. I love you all more than words can say.

Acknowledgements and appreciation go also to my beautiful Freedom Team:

Kelly Fuller, aka The Zoo Keeper, who listens with loving ears, and is always willing to go for hikes in the human washing machine (Nature);

Laurie Larson, aka The Money Magnet, who always pushes me to stand in more of who I am, and steps out of her comfort zone, and jumps in with both feet, and remembers;

John Schaefer, aka The Wizard, for courageously stepping into his role in this awakening, who is always supportive and never afraid to speak his truth;

Jennifer Hough, for having the courage to stand in who she is, and for creating the space so I could meet my beautiful soul family. And for literally covering my butt;

Susan Crossman, a brilliant book writing coach who teased the experiences out of me: without her I would never have completed this powerful journey of sharing *Naked and Awake*. She is an amazing conduit for change in her own gift of interpreting experiences and downloads, assisting in translating them into words that are easily understood by all of humanity, a spectacular editor, and someone I am proud to call my friend and soul family;

Brooke Clodfelter my sister from another mister, for listening with loving ears while I had melt-downs along the way, for holding space for me to fully integrate even more of who I am, and for simply being the best friend anyone could ask for;

Sherryl Lin for all her love and assistance;

Bonnie Serratore, for courageously leading the way on a path less traveled, allowing me to step in to my gifts more fully;

My publisher, Michael Davie and Manor House, for bringing my dream to fruition and publishing my book.

A special shout out goes to Andre Klasen for not taking no for an answer, and for pushing me to say yes to a session!;

To all the amazing courageous clients I have had the honor and privilege to work with, (you know who you are), I love and appreciate all of you;

To all my friends, who bring such joy to my life;

And most of all, to you, my readers, for having the courage to question if there is more available to you, and for taking a step towards your FREEDOM. I am so grateful for YOU! I see you! You are so loved! You matter and you are more than enough!

A heartfelt thank you to all!

Peace be with you.

- **Kaayla Vedder**, Freedom Accelerator!

Table of Contents

Praise for Naked & Awake

"Kaayla Vedder serves up opportunities for readers to see their lives in new and empowering ways while opening a doorway into the mysterious dimensions that lay beyond the everyday. Written with warmth and compassion for our human journey, *Naked and Awake* is the perfect kick-start for anyone who is yearning to reclaim the amazing life that awaits, just beyond the rules they are using to keep joy confined."
- **Susan Crossman**, author, *Passages to Epiphany*

"Naked and Awake is full of pearls of wisdom; it is a reminder for some, and an awakening for others that we are all Creators and Divine Beings in a human body. Kaayla is witty, charming, authentic and fun. Her sharing is heartfelt, her intention to raise consciousness is evident, and her desire for the liberation of humanity comes forth in her work and her writing."
- **Bonnie Serratore**, Master Accelerator, Spiritual Acceleration

"As experienced from a journey of fear into love, Kaayla Vedder shares *Naked and Awake,* a straight forward and personally candid, conversational presentation of the many ways in which archaic thought forms, emotions, actions and reactions may be viewed in a new openness to bring forth the freedom of remembering and awakening to the brilliant love that you are; creator expressing throughout your life-stream as creator incarnate, the expression of love in a very light state."
- **William Linville,** Creator Consciousness, Universalis

"As the new era dawns and our World Family is welcomed as the Galactic Citizens we've long been, Kaayla has penned a primer for this age; ripe with experiential wisdom, brimming with vision and intention, Kaayla issues a timely plea: Wake Up! I dare you to read this book and NOT feel an abundance of hope, gratitude, inspiration, and fearlessness..."
- **John Wright Schaefer**, Peyton Wright Gallery

"Why do I self-sabotage my success? Kaayla uncovered limiting beliefs that I'm not worthy or deserving of abundance and acknowledgement. Now I can dissolve them and enjoy a balanced rich life. My childhood experiences and various relationships into my 20s conditioned me to have these beliefs. I also believe energy at a spiritual level of my being and my universe also contributed to my daily life behaviours. Kaayla has a profound connection to energy, spectrum's and entities that allow her to see things that most of us cannot. I am so grateful for what she does and for the wisdom that she channels into our world. Her book, activation's and events are a blessing. Thank you Kaayla."
- **Justin McMakin**, Vision Discovery Facilitator

"A Healer and Freedom Accelerator, committed to ending suffering, anxiety, stress, illness, and injury, She serves the world as a pathway to connect people to their higher-self. Through Kaayla, one releases energetic entanglements, entities and limiting beliefs to achieve true Freedom."
- **The Universe**

Foreword

Everything had come to a standstill. The cool tang of pine lay sharp upon the morning air and the sun radiated down on a perfect spring morning. Raindrops glistened on the rocks and trees around me and the stillness of Nature seeped into my soul. I was sure I could feel the leaves breathing and the rocks listening.

I stood there, my arms lifted to the sky, and my head thrown back in reverent gratitude. And I breathed so deeply that I felt as though the air was surging through my body and out the soles of my feet, down into the rocks and loam of an ancient landmass, tying me to the centre of the Earth and tethering me to my purpose on the planet. That moment of perfection uplifted me as it humbled me and I thought, "If only everyone could feel this way. If only everyone could *live* this way."

This book is part of my answer to that quest.

Once up on a time in my life I lived in a cloud of anxiety so debilitating that I sometimes wondered how I was going to make it through yet another day. It had a lot to do with living against the grain of the person I was truly put on the planet to be, and a lot to do with denying my own right to live joyfully within my own skin.

I was w-a-a-a-y out of alignment.

And if you are reading this book, maybe you can relate to how that feels. Over time, I found the assistance I needed to take those challenging steps back to me, and I learned how to integrate love and joy and wonder back into my life.

I was surprised to learn along the way that the anxiety had been a friend, not a foe, in that it had triggered my search for something better, something wonderful, that I now find regularly in my walks in Nature in my own backyard, and everywhere else in my life, too.

I wrote this book to help you find your way along that path, too.

I've been a healer of sorts for many years and, for, a lot of that time, I enthusiastically investigated and experienced many different healing modalities as I tried to find a context for what it is that I do. I also wanted to figure out what I should call my business. I mean, really, to quote that great line from the song in the movie *The Sound of Music*, I might as well be trying to "catch a cloud."

There didn't seem to be a name that summarized my process and provided my clients with a framework for understanding how I was assisting them. Despite years of searching, I never did find what I was looking for, although I obtained many different tools for my tool kit.

I was sitting at my computer one day, having another go at the problem, when suddenly the word "Kripa" popped into my awareness. I thought, "I've never heard of that word before, I wonder what it means?"

I grabbed my dictionary and discovered that it's about a release or a rebirth from the karmic journey. It's about disentangling from prior lifetimes so you can embrace the fullness of what is available to you. I realized I don't need to have somebody physically in front of me when I work with them – I can do what I do anywhere — and suddenly I had my business name: Kripa Quantum Healing. Thank you, Universe!

Writing this book has been full of those moments – I'd download floods of words from the universal "word-tank in the sky" and sift through them as my book coach and I engaged ourselves in the challenging adventure of creating an enlightening adventure for my readers to enjoy.

Each chapter in this book reflects a topic that I found important or interesting on my own journey towards releasing anxiety, and I've included plenty of "Freedom Tips" to help you disentangle yourself from whatever Karmic concept you believe — incorrectly, I might add —is holding you back.

Writing this book has been challenging, rewarding, terrifying, fun, exciting, daunting and a whole lot of other things besides.

It has stretched my bandwidth and twanged my heart-strings. And, more than anything, it has shown me, yet again, that we live in the embrace of a loving Universe that is always there, always *here,* and always ours.

I invite you to read this book with an open mind and an open heart.

You might find some of what I share odd and, if that's the case, then I invite you to withhold judgement.

Scientists are finding more strange things about our world all the time, and even electricity would have seemed impossible to someone living 300 years ago.

If you read this book with a growing feeling of "Yes, Yes, *YES!*" then I invite you to rejoice in the fact that you've found another member of your Tribe, someone else who "gets it," knows it and lives it.

You are never alone.

My story:

I grew up in a house where I could see, feel and hear energy. My earliest memory is when I was three years old seeing dead people in my room and at the time I didn't know that's what they were. I recall telling my parents and them asking me what they looked like.

Now, at age three, you really don't have much to reference other than cartoons so I said one of them kinda looks like Popeye and so on; my parents were truly trying to help and decided to fix the apparent problem I was no longer allowed to watch cartoons. As a result of this response I just stopped talking about it. This was the first step of my shutting down.

When in elementary school I was bullied because as most of us know, kids are amazing shit detectors. They can sense when someone or something is different than them.

As much as I tried to fit into society I just couldn't get my square peg being to fit in that round hole. As a result I became very angry and toughened up. Fights were common in my school years.

At age 15 I understood that entities were trying to affect my life and I was scared, and feeling really alone and helpless.

I reached out to many religious leaders in the community only to be told that I was possessed by the devil.

A part of me knew this was an untruth however after many weeks of resisting and battling this entity I just couldn't do it anymore. I walked up to my mom and told her I was crazy and that she needed to put me in a home.

Luckily, my mom was a very open-minded person and at some point in her life a woman had told her that one of her girls was going to require some assistance with her gifts.

She brought in a woman who channeled energy who assisted me immensely. I realized I wasn't crazy. I was still unwilling to embrace what I experienced and as a result shut off my ability to see what I had been seeing.

Unfortunately, I could still feel it, which proved frustrating in the coming years. I can recall my parents laughing at how quickly I would get to anger.

I was feeling so misunderstood and alone. I can recall thinking what is wrong with people? Why are they so mean to one another?

I became whoever people thought I should be and I married my high school sweetheart who knew nothing of my experiences. The marriage lasted less than a year.

Years later I settled into another marriage feeling that this must be as good as it gets. Another unhealthy marriage, but I had two beautiful girls. I knew I had to assist my children, who had started to hear and see the same things I used to.

It was time to stand in who I am and own it. That was the beginning of me remembering all of my amazing super powers that I came in with. However, I still didn't say anything to anyone, because I didn't want to be judged again.

In 2007 I became very ill. Western medicine was unable to diagnose anything specific other than nothing was working well together however nothing was bad enough to remove.

I released 40 pounds in 30 days and my body had begun to eat my muscle. Doctors didn't know what to do. I was dying.

I knew I couldn't follow traditional means to heal... so I didn't... I followed my guidance.

In the last 10 years, I have realized who I am; I am a seer and energy conduit and a guide for people to remember who they really are, and live out their purpose. I know that I am here to assist people who know they too have a purpose, but they don't know how to get past the stuff that stops them... and they've tried.

I am inspired to use what I have learned and the abilities I was given to help others to thrive instead of just survive.

So, read this book, embrace who you are, and then maybe go out into nature, throw your head back, and breathe as though the air were surging through your body and out the soles of your feet, down into the rocks and loam of an ancient landmass, tying you to the centre of the Earth and tethering you to your purpose on the planet.

Release your fear, release your anxiety and let this book help you come home to who you truly are.

Love Bombs

- Kaayla Vedder

Introduction

I have to admit that I wrote this book almost by accident. I've never considered myself a "writer," although I write comfortably enough for the various needs of my business.

For most of my life, I never had a burning urge to put my thoughts together into a book. Like a lot of other people, I've had friends tell me I should write a book someday, but I always kind of laughed the idea off and said, "Yeah, right."

So, it came as something of a surprise when the Universe conspired to bring me both the opportunity and the desire to make this book happen.

The project has taken me way out of my comfort zone at times, and the support of my writing coach and editor, Susan Crossman, has been key.

But what's really driven me onward has been my desire to create a space where people can relate to their lives in new ways and recognize that they're not crazy.

I realized that we are all living in paradigms that often don't serve us, and my own journey of awakening has brought me to focus extensively on shifting paradigms to improve my world, and the worlds of my clients.

I think of this book as a kind of conversation. Each chapter is a topic you and I might discuss while sitting at my kitchen table over a cup of tea, with the mountain winds blowing cheerfully around the house and the dog sitting comfortably at our feet.

Be warned that I don't want to talk about the weather. I don't want to gossip about what people are wearing. I want to talk about things that make me wonder, about the subtext of our lives and families, about the things that have happened to us and the meaning we have taken from them.

Like a lot of people in the 21st Century, I used to struggle with a lot of debilitating anxiety. I didn't realize at the time that it was the Universe's way of compelling me to look deeper, to truly own my gifts and live my life in alignment with who I truly was.

Anxiety was actually there to guide me into the flow: I wasn't paying attention to my inner compass and I was living life on other people's terms. I wasn't looking after myself and I was unhappily married. I wasn't getting huge satisfaction from my employment.

My hopes and dreams were irrelevant in the context of my own life, and my body was reacting by breaking down on me. Everything was a mess. That started me on a journey of awakening.

Ever since I can remember, I have always been aware of the place of energy in my life but this life can be a process of forgetting who we are as well. I did leave my husband and start a new life, but I was still learning how to take care of myself. When an illness hit me with its full force, I was at a place in life where I had set my understanding of energy aside.

I was focused on what was in front of me, I was operating from a place of fear and "not enough."

As well, I was focused on what I saw and heard, rather than what *could be*. Western medicine was unable to diagnose or solve the problems I was experiencing; I was dying.

I was finally referred to a homeopathic doctor and began treatments with him.

I also began working on my physical body myself, and I came to learn a lot about the levels of vibrations in and around my body.

Finally, I was able to clear energy blocks in my physical body, as well as in other levels of my being.

During this time, I was reunited with a man I have known since I was six years old.

I did everything I could to get him to run away but he stuck around and gave me the space to be completely myself.

We married in August, 2010, and since then I've become more comfortable in standing in all of who I am and why I am here, using my gifts with energy, and also being fully supportive of myself.

I've been able to clear and remove many past life issues that were affecting my current life. And I've embraced life with vigor and delight.

Be aware that much of the information in this book will come in at subconscious levels.

There are activations and encodements included in these words that will assist you, as well as me, in releasing the density from all of humanity.

These "downloads" are like beautiful delicious balls of light that come into your being and open up and become a part of who you are to assist you when necessary.

I stepped out of the anxiety when I stepped into who I am and started to stand up for what was important to me. I made different choices and watched the petals of a whole different life flower in front of me.

I will be sharing a lot of personal stories in this book, stories that put me out there, naked, in front of the entire world. These stories contain a lot of the wisdom that has brought me peace.

If you're reading this book, it's my wish that you feel renewed and encouraged by the end of it, and that you feel more prepared to take your place among those of us who are here to raise the vibration of all humanity.

I invite you to remember and embrace who you truly are. If you've gone through your life learning how to live in a place of fear, then

As well, I invite you to release yourself from those shackles of fear and remember yourself as a spark of divinity.

The Universe could have made a rainbow or a galaxy or a diamond the moment you arrived on the planet. Instead, it made you.

You are not alone.

I invite you to recognize and embrace the basic fact that you are not your stories and that you don't have to keep on reliving them over and over or experiencing the perceptively negative feelings they have generated.

You can shift your story and the vibration it sets up within you. You might benefit from some assistance with that. But it can be done.

And by the way, may I remind you that you don't have to assist anyone else on their journey?

When you look after you, the world will open up for others, as well.

While you are reading this book, I encourage you to check in with how you feel.

You don't have to understand all of what's happening for you in this world or, in fact, all of the emotions that this book might stir up within you.

My hope is that this book will help you to experience whatever comes up so it can move through you.

I urge my clients to recognize that emotions are for experiencing: they are not meant to be held onto and examined and judged. Let them go and let yourself be all of who you came here to be.

FREEDOM TIP #1:

If you think you know everything, and you walk around saying "I know, I know," and you're fighting to convince others that you're correct, and you're right, you've just shut yourself off from knowing more. Try saying this instead: "If I know *this* much about this topic, I wonder how much more I *don't* know?"

Chapter One: Get Off My Yoga Mat!

Breathe it in... the greatest act of love is to witness and love another and their journey, regardless of what you think it should look like.

- Kaayla Vedder

Do your friends and loved ones sometimes drive you nuts?

Do you see all kinds of things you feel they are doing "incorrectly" or inefficiently, or do you worry about some of their behaviours so much that sometimes it feels like you're going to be ill? Do you just want to step in and fix things for them so you can save them the agony of their own mis-steps?

Be careful that you aren't trying to carry them.

There's a difference between "carrying" people and "caring for" them. Carrying people is about taking responsibility for the results that they're generating by their own actions.

It's about taking charge, fixing, organizing, and otherwise doing things so they're done the perceptively "right" way. In a way, though, when you carry someone you are insulating them from their own results. Carrying someone makes the assumption that they can't look after themselves. And that's a very disempowering assumption.

Better yet is the idea of "caring for" someone. Caring for someone is about generously allowing them to experience the consequences of their own behaviour in the full expectation that, since the Universe has their back, they don't need you to step in and take over.

They're *already being looked after* by a force that is so much more powerful and all-knowing than you can possibly attempt to be. It's all God.

We Each Have Our Own Yoga Mat

You can imagine the misery that would result if you went to a yoga class and started trying to do yoga on someone else's mat — or if someone tried to do their poses on your mat. What a disaster! Life is like that, too. We each have our own metaphorical yoga mat and there just isn't room for more than one person on that mat! You can live your own life and let your loved ones live theirs.

A friend of mine was married to a man who was often angry and she carried him a lot. She did countless little things to make sure everything ran smoothly for him because she didn't want to deal with his anger. But here's the thing: he was always angry anyway. She eventually left him, and one day she asked her kids if they ever wished their mommy and daddy were still together. She was surprised when her oldest daughter said "Yes!"

"Really, why would you wish that?" my friend asked. And the answer floored her:

"Because then Daddy wouldn't be yelling at *us* all the time," my little Sweet Pea said. "He'd be yelling at *you*."

My friend had thought that her ex would change. While she was in the marriage, she had thought that he was just angry with her, and she thought that things would get better after they split. By ending the marriage, she had stopped carrying him, and she had stopped carrying the responsibility for the entire relationship. That allowed her to release an enormous amount of stress, anxiety and unhappiness. It allowed her to start to look after herself and her kids in healthy ways. It didn't mean he started to take responsibility for his actions, however, as witnessed by the fact that he yelled at his kids a lot.

Here's another example of how carrying works. My mom took a bad fall one day and she said: "I feel so bad about making everyone worry." Well, that's one way of looking at it.

"You don't make everyone worry," I said. "It's their choice to worry about you or not. I don't worry about you, I simply love you."

Worrying is About Carrying

Worrying is about carrying. Loving is about caring. You can't have worry and love in the same space: one is fear-based and one is love-based. If you're worrying about someone, you're creating even more things to worry about. My mother was very busy judging herself and being hard on herself. When, really, this was an opportunity for everyone to care about her, rather than to carry her.

One experiment you can do to get a sense of how much you are "carrying" rather than "caring" is to stop and be the observer for a while. I went out for a coffee with a friend a while ago and did this very thing.

And boy, was it challenging! When you agree to observe and not judge, you put yourself in the position of being able to choose your response to other people's stuff.

My friend had recently had some redirects from the Universe and she was unable to work. We've had conversations before where I've tried to leap to her assistance and do whatever I could to make her world better.

On this one particular visit, where I was just observing and not responding, she told me about how she had seen people shopping at the Salvation Army store, which is a low-price second hand store, and she was outraged to see a couple of people who owned other second hand shops wheeling through the aisles with full shopping carts. My friend felt it was wrong for these people to buy clothes at a low price and then sell them at a higher price. She perceived that these people were taking something away from her.

In previous conversations, I might have leapt in and tried to make her feel better about herself and her situation – to carry her emotionally, in other words. But in that moment, I was observing her non-judgmentally, and I decided to ask her to consider another possibility.

I mentioned to her that my husband had purchased some product from a store that was going out of business, and it turned out that he had purchased more product than his business required. He then sold the extra product at a fair price, however at a slightly higher price than his company had paid for the goods. "Was he taking something away from someone else?" I asked.

"That's different," my friend said.

I asked if she would be willing to see that the people who went out finding clothes to re-sell were actually doing work that others would be willing to pay extra for, so they didn't have to do that work. The energy shifted and my friend became very upset with me; our visit ended on that note.

We carry ourselves, too, by the way. When we make excuses for our situation and let ourselves "off the hook" on promises we've made to ourselves to reach farther or expand outward, we are carrying ourselves. It's a way of keeping ourselves small and it's like making the assumption that we probably can't get where we want to go or achieve what we would like to achieve. Balderdash! The Universe has your back and you deserve to evolve.

Observe with Compassion

I was able to look at my friend's entire situation with compassion, and I realized that up until that conversation, I had been an enabler in her life. When the fear of not having enough had crept into her world in the past, I had not been of assistance: I had commiserated with her, and jumped in, and tried to change her circumstances. I had carried her. It was all very interesting. In deciding to *not* carry her, I was giving her the opportunity to see the world a different way. How she reacted to my position was not my responsibility, much as I was sorry it brought disharmony into the relationship.

Are you carrying someone as well? I double dog dare you to spend an entire day being the observer in your relationships...when you notice yourself starting to judge someone or their situation, let go of judging yourself for judging: simply notice it and let it go with love…and continue being the observer.

What if instead of getting upset and coming from a place of lack and fear, we are able to look at the entire bigger picture and simply trust that our higher levels (God, the Universe, divine grace, Jesus, all the ascended masters your guides and angels and whoever else you might have on your spiritual team) have got your back? When we are fearful, our ego and our judgments of others have a great time beating us down.

What if we could blow apart the paradigm of being a victim, or the paradigm of lack? How amazing would it be if you could live your life in the flow of what is presenting and know that your higher levels are supporting you? What if you could live your life without fear? What if you could live your life in total trust and fluidity?

The Value of Vibration

Our vibration is like the frequency of a radio station or a channel: it vibrates at its own unique level – higher or lower don't equate to better or less than, they are just different.

When I say frequency, I mean that the more "awake" you become, the more aware you become of your ego, your logical mind, and the spiritual being of you. You become more neutral with life in general and you stop carrying people so much. You allow yourself to be completely vulnerable in certain situations.

The more you stand in who you are, the more your frequency rises because you're truly trusting the Universe and you're getting that there is a much bigger plan for you than what you can see in front of your face. And if that's true for you, it's true for everyone. Which means you can care without carrying. They're going to be just fine. And so are you.

The Call to Source

I am not a scientist so you will have to Google your way through exploring this, but it has been scientifically proven that each cell in our body is its own entity. Every single cell that makes up your body is of The One. And we are joined in our humanity and in our divinity.

Sometimes, when we are called to experience sadness, we witness it change from pity or sorrow to divine love, and sometimes that makes us weep from a place of love, love for the person or situation that triggered our emotions. We hold that divine love for them, and we feel gratitude for the fact that they are on this journey with us.

We weep for the emotions that we are experiencing, but also for all of humanity. And in so doing we assist in the shifting of the density that has entangled human experiences for many life times in the effort to keep us "safe."

We are already safe. There is no need to carry other people – they, too, are already safe. Stay on your own yoga mat and don't invite people onto it with you!

I invite you to ask yourself these questions:

- Where have you carried others — or yourself — in your life?

- Where do you see that you are carrying others in your life now?

FREEDOM TIP #2:

Imagine the infinity symbol as a golden honey-like nectar flowing in the shape of a figure 8... place yourself in one of the circles and place the person or people who you are carrying in the other circle. This creates a fluid circle of unity and divine love around each of you, which allows you to totally support them without carrying them.

FREEDOM TIP #3:

Hold a space of love without expectation or judgement of what another person may be experiencing. Practise the art of not carrying them, so you can create a comfortable place for growth and love. Hold the space with love.

Chapter 2: Out of Control and Loving It!

Attention Please:

The Vice President of the Universe has called to say he'd really like his job back. He says that no matter how hard you try to plan your future, you just can't come close to putting in place all of the intricate puzzle pieces that the Universe has at its disposal. Stop micro-managing your life!

- Kaayla Vedder

Isn't it funny how often we believe that we have a much better plan for our lives than the one the Creator of the entire freaking Universe is presenting to us in every single moment? How arrogant and presumptuous that is!

There has been a lot of ink spilled over the past decade or so on the topic of the Law of Attraction. Many of us have come to believe that if we just think the right thoughts, visualize the right visions, and vibrate just the right way, we will get what we want.

There is nothing wrong with the Law of Attraction. It's just that it's not the whole story. It's great to be specific about what you would like in life...just add the words "or better" to the description and then be open to what presents.

Your life is not going to look like you think it should. I invite you to let go of that idea, to be out of control and loving it — and enjoy the ride.

33

Here are a few examples of people who set out to direct their lives, only to find that the "Or Better" showed up to surprise them:

Charles Darwin was not hell-bent on becoming a scientist his whole life, thanks to his dad, who called him lazy and too dreamy. Darwin once wrote, "I was considered by all my masters and my father, a very ordinary boy, rather below the common standard of intellect."

Walt Disney was fired from a job at the Kansas City Star newspaper in 1919 because, his editor said, he "lacked imagination and had no good ideas."

Thomas Edison used to conduct experiments in secret while working at Western Union...until, one night in 1867, some acid he had spilled ate through the entire floor. He was fired and subsequently decided to pursue inventing full time.

Bill Gates dropped out of Harvard to start a business with Paul Allen called Traf-O-Data. It flopped. Luckily, they tried their hand at business again, and this time Microsoft was born.

Stephen King's first and most renowned book, Carrie, was rejected 30 times. King decided to toss the book. His wife then went through the trash to rescue it and convinced him to re-submit it one more time.

Marilyn Monroe was told by modeling agencies when she was trying to start her career that she should consider becoming a secretary.

Elvis Presley was told by the concert hall manager at Nashville's Grand Ole Opry after performing there that he was better off returning to Memphis and driving trucks (his former career).

JK Rowling, author of the famed Harry Potter series of books, got fired from her job at the London office of Amnesty International because she wrote stories on her work computer all day.

Oprah Winfrey was fired from her job as an evening news reporter because she apparently couldn't sever her emotions from her stories.

Did you notice how each of those individuals set out to accomplish one thing and ended up with a redirect that took them in an entirely new direction, one for which they are now justifiably famous?

And, probably at the time of their redirect, each one of them felt disappointed, devastated, angry or hurt that the plan they had made had fallen apart. Although we are not all celebrities, billionaires, creative geniuses or famous scientists, this is happening in the life of each and every one of us, every minute of every day.

But we tend to overthink our lives. We get paralyzed by mind chatter.

FREEDOM TIP #4:

The Universe has a plan, however it is up to you to move energy on things, to see if what you're considering "grows legs," If you see a job and you think, "Wow! I would love to do that!" and then your ego starts telling you how you're not qualified, it's not close enough to home, they probably won't offer the hours you require blah blah blah... Apply anyway! See what happens. If it's not in the highest for you at this time, it either won't come to fruition or it will simply fall apart.

Mind Chatter

Our identities are quite often running our show—have you ever had the feeling, for example, that you have to figure it all out? That you have to "get it right," or plan endlessly to make sure you get the outcome you desire? That requires that you take a lot of action and strategically wrestle your world to the ground, right? Isn't that a lot of work?

Consider instead that the Universe has already figured it all out for you. That everything has been planned, organized, rectified, perfected and put in motion, and all you have to do is be receptive.

The Universe may not give you the answer you're looking for, and you might not get the results you thought you wanted. But everything will unfold smoothly in a moment...in the flow...through a phone call...a surprise email...a chance meeting...a detour...a mix-up...a "mistake"...an illness, or more. Things don't look like you thought they were supposed to look. And they are perfect anyway.

Yes, it's all coming together. Just stop overthinking everything, put a sock in the mind chatter and know that everything is completely OK. Everything can change in a heartbeat. And does. And will.

Here's an idea: Give your mind a job to keep it from getting in your way all the time...stop everything just for a few moments. Close your eyes and tell your mind to pay attention to your breath. Repeat as needed.

Have you ever been late for something? No matter what you did to make up for lost time, you were still late. You had your partner drop the kids off at school, did your makeup in the car, took a shortcut, exceeded the speed limit and prayed. And you were still late. How was that happening *for* you? Well, maybe you avoided being involved in a tragic car accident or maybe you ended up meeting someone you never would have met otherwise. We can only see so much with the limited human radar we've been given, and there is far more going on than you can possibly know.

You actually aren't in control of your entire life, although of course you have free will to make choices. The Universe has much more in store for you than you can possibly imagine and it is working tirelessly to create a world where everything happens *for* you, not *to* you. Trust that the Universe has your back...Always!

FREEDOM TIP #5:

The Universe always has your back. When you start to say yes to everything that is presenting in your life, it opens up so many more ways for the Universe to deliver what you want and better! Say YES! You can't get it wrong.

A Christmas Story

This was beyond anything we could have imagined. It was Christmas Eve, an amazing night, with all the kids from our melded family getting along wonderfully and truly enjoying each other. The mother of my husband, Bryan, was there with her "man friend," as she calls him, along with my mom and my two girls, Bryan's two boys and his daughter, everyone's significant others, and our new grandbaby boy. We all exchanged gifts and warm hugs and then had a delicious German Christmas dinner of European wieners and warm potato salad.

We were all sitting around the very large dining room table and laughing at something — you know, the kind of laughter that is contagious? The kind of laughter that makes your face and belly hurt. Our melded family has amazing humor and things can get very out of hand very quickly. As we continued to laugh, all the kids began commenting on Bryan's color. He looked like he was turning burgundy, which made us all laugh even harder, and as we laughed, I told him to keep breathing.

All of the kids had gotten together and had a group photo taken of themselves, and they had framed it for our gift. As you can imagine, trying to bring two separate families together into a harmonious new entity is challenging, and we'd had our share of struggle in finding ways to make our family work. This gift was evidence of a dream come true. Bryan and I both had tears in our eyes when we opened the gift: we had given up hoping for any particular outcome regarding how things might or might not come together. All in all, this was a wonderful night. By 10:00 p.m., the last of the company had headed home.

I went to our shared office, which is just off our garage, to make some last-minute tags for gifts that were going under the tree for Christmas morning. That's when my side of the family would celebrate the season. Stockings would be dumped out and squeals of laughter would ring throughout the house as the gifts would be opened. Then we would have a wonderful breakfast followed by a big turkey dinner.

I had my back to the office door as I sat at my desk reflecting on the evening's events, and I was smiling in gratitude. I heard the door to the garage open and I knew someone was going to come through the office door. I heard my husband in a very soft struggling voice say "Honey, I feel funny."

I had a flashback to a vision I'd had months earlier: In that vision I'd heard my husband say those exact words, in that same voice: "Honey, I feel funny." At the time of the vision I was shown that he was having a heart attack but because I couldn't see him in the vision, I had assumed he had been talking to me over the phone. As a result, I had always made sure that I had his address handy whenever he was out of town. I swung around and told him to sit in his office chair. His skin was grey and he had both his hands on his chest. I already had the phone in my hand, waiting for 911 to answer.

When the operator answered, I said I needed an ambulance right away. We spoke in code, so Bryan wouldn't know what was going on, and we came to the conclusion that my husband was having a massive heart attack. While we waited for the ambulance, Bryan, kept saying "it hurts so bad." Bryan's a big guy and I'm no pansy, but I told him that if he had to lie down to do it now because I wouldn't be able to get him on the floor. He said "I'm fine here."

Just then the operator asked me if he was still conscious. I said "yes," and she asked if I had an aspirin; I didn't. And with that, Bryan suddenly announced that he was going to lay down on the floor. He literally fell out of his chair and hit the floor with a full-frontal crash. I told the operator what had happened and she said to let her know if he went unconscious.

"How much longer until the ambulance gets here?" I asked. She said it was on its way, and within seconds I heard the sirens. I dropped the phone and ran out to open the big garage door.

The air was crisp and cold on my face but it felt good, ushering in the relief of assistance as it did.

Everything seemed to be taking place in slow motion as the ambulance backed into the driveway. I showed the two paramedics into the office. One took me aside and told me to go gather Bryan's medical card and my purse.

Bryan was loaded into the ambulance and they pulled away with lights and sirens blaring. I hopped up into my big silver truck and quickly pulled out of the driveway. Everything felt surreal. My body was freaking out—I could feel myself shaking from the inside out. My hands were trembling, and my mind was replaying all the events of the evening.

When I arrived at the hospital, all the doctors and nurses were scurrying around Bryan getting readouts, taking blood, talking with him. It was like organized chaos. They had all done this before. Bryan, ever the smart ass, was busy making jokes. "Whatever that spray was that they gave me under my tongue has totally worked," he said. "I think I can go home."

One of the doctors turned and looked at me. Then he said, "I know it seems like it would be a good thing that the spray worked, however it actually means he may have damage to his heart. We will be taking him to Royal Columbian hospital about an hour from here to see a specialist."

FREEDOM TIP #6:

Worrying is like praying for what you don't want. Stop, take a breath, and get into calmness. Focus on what you want…really feel it, experience it in your cells, and be open to something even better.

In a Daze

Bryan was in danger of dying. I held his hand as they prepared him for the ride.

"I'm scared," he said.

"I know you are," I replied. "Do you want to live?"

"Yes," he said.

"Then continue to say 'I live,' and see yourself coming back to me."

They took him away and the nurse told me she would call me when they were on their way back. "I should be calling in about three hours," she said.

I went home in a daze, feeling weird and unsettled. I told my girls what was going on and I called Bryan's ex-wife, sharing some tears with her in hopes of a good outcome.

I had no idea if I would see my husband alive again.

I began going over all the wonderful things we had done together and I just couldn't stop crying.

I lay in bed waiting for my phone to ring; it had been four hours since he had left, going on for a fifth.

I was about to call the hospital when my phone rang.

It was the nurse calling from the ambulance. She told me that Bryan had had two stents put into his heart and that I could meet him at the hospital in 30 minutes. He was doing great. Wow!

It truly was the best Christmas gift ever. Bryan had survived. His body was talking to him, letting him know that things had to move and change. This is called the Cosmic Two-by-Four. It smacked him down and gave him the opportunity to make changes in his life so he could engage more fully in a healthy self.

The massive heart attack had been a symptom of what had been going on inside his body. It turned out to be his second chance at life.

This is not what either of us had wanted to happen.

It's not what we'd set out to invite into our lives.

We didn't "manifest" a heart attack. The Universe engineered it, in collaboration with Bryan's higher levels.

What it gave us was a chance to get along even better than before and appreciate, to a much greater extent than ever, our existence in each other's lives.

It gave Bryan the chance to honour his body more than he had been.

And, it let us understand how great a gift it is to have a second chance at life.

I have a friend who went through a similar experience, in which her husband died.

At that time, her world had fallen apart and there didn't seem to be a single thing good about being left a widow with young children to raise.

But within a few years, she had pulled her life back together, reignited her business interests, started to take a huge amount of joy in her work and realized how much richer her life was because of this second opportunity to follow her career interests.

Her children are doing great and life has opened up for all of them.

These are scary experiences, to be sure. Some of them, like mine, have what we consider "happy endings" and some of them perceptively do not.

In my case, I was given the chance to reflect, yet again, upon the miracle of being looked after to such a degree that even if Bryan *had* passed away, I would know that it was still in the highest (best interests) for both of us for that outcome to occur.

FREEDOM TIP #7:

As soon as you let go of your expectations around what you think things should look like, the answer will come, and it might not look anything like what you in particular, or society in general, thinks it should. Run with it anyway.

Chapter Three: Cha-Ching! Tapping Into Your Cosmic Bank Account

What you focus on, and believe in, expands through every cell of your being, and creates your reality... The Universe always blesses you with abundance.

Your universal bank account is overflowing with everything you could desire, and more. So, you might be wondering where all your goodies are? You just have to be ready to receive them.

When you put your order in to the "kitchen" of the Universe, say "thank you." And trust that you might not get exactly what you asked for. It will be better — so release any resistance to it.

The proper response for anything that shows up is "thank you," even if what shows up isn't what you perceptively thought you wanted.

There are many aspects to this issue of abundance.

Many of us want what we want when we want it. And sometimes we have to wait.

Bryan and I put our order in to the Universe for a house that was exactly like the one we ended up buying. But we had to wait almost 18 months for it to show up.

We wanted a big house that was a turnkey situation – we didn't want to do any construction, even though my husband is a general contractor and knows how to do just about everything. The house we ultimately bought had sat empty for over a year and it was well within our budget.

It took a whole lot of stuff happening way beyond what we could see at the time for the purchase to fall into place. It happened in divine timing, not our timing: although we were ready to move long before we actually did, our order wasn't ready when we were and, in the meantime, we didn't settle for something else that wasn't right for us.

It helped confirm for me the importance of trusting that everything is happening in perfect divine timing – everything is assisting you to getting to the vibration where you're a match for what you've ordered up.

FREEDOM TIP #8:

When you put your order into the universal kitchen, you may have to wait so the Universe can get everything into place for your specific order. If you keep changing your order, it's like changing your order for a cook in a restaurant kitchen: it will take longer.

Fried Computer, Anyone?

Here's another example: I was going to take my kids to the store in the new car that had recently showed up for us, and as I was getting ready to go, my computer burned out on me. It was completely fried. I went to our favourite computer shop and said that I needed a computer that could do this, this and this.

The salesperson at the computer shop said "Yes, but it's going to cost you $1,400. I thought about it, tuned in, and asked my guides if it was in the highest for me to get that computer. I got a "yes." I ordered it and, later that day, headed out of town for three days. While I was gone, Bryan forwarded an email from my accountant.

That email showed what my tax rebate was going to be: $1,400. If it hadn't been in my highest to get the computer, something would have happened to make the transaction difficult. The store would have been out of stock, the model I wanted would have been discontinued or some other calamity would have come up to put the sale off. I didn't sit and worry about how I was going to pay for this computer – I knew it would work itself out.

This kind of thing happens all the time. When we let it.

M-O-N-E-Y is a Five-Letter Word

The question of abundance is an issue for many people, although a lot of folks don't want to talk about that five-letter word, M-O-N-E-Y. We think that somehow the amount of money someone has defines who they are and how successful or worthy they are. I answered my phone yesterday and had a great conversation with a man who was following up on a program that I apparently had looked into at some point last year. The program was about making gobs of money, millionaire-level money, with residual income, etc. I listened to what he had to say and answered a lot of questions he had about my finances. I was still getting a YES to continue the conversation.

I asked him a few questions:

Q. 1.   "Are you a millionaire?"

A. 1.   "I was, however I am not now," he said. He proceeded to tell me this huge story about his life. He was still very plugged in to his story about how others had treated him and how deceitful they all had been.

Q. 2.   "Do you see now how everything happened *for* you and not *to* you?"

A. 2.   "Yes, my wife and I have much more appreciation and gratitude for everything in our lives. We've started a non-profit charity and it is starting to thrive..."

He went on to ask me if I was happy with where I am in my personal and business life.

"YES, I am so happy," I said. "Everything is coming together in divine timing, I need nothing and desire many things. How could I be anything else? If I were un-happy with where things are, I would bring more of that to me. It's all happening in divine timing and there is so much more that is on its way to me."

Although I got a YES to take the call, when I tuned in to my higher levels I got a No to a Yes to the program this man was offering. I say "Yes" when things present and continue to tune in to see if it's still a" yes." Until it's a "No."

When you say YES to what presents, it provides the Universe so many more ways to come in and deliver answers to your questions, sometimes questions you didn't even know you had.

Sometimes, it's a way for the Universe to validate where you are on your journey and how much you have to be grateful for.

Oh, I almost forgot: when I was on the phone with this man, my husband dropped the mail on my desk and I received a cheque. Thank you, Universe!

Be Willing to Receive

You've put it out to the Universe that you would like to get something and you're ready to really let it go and let God/the Universe do his or her work…are you also open to *receiving* what's coming your way? If you're not open to receive — like you're one of these people who says "I've got this handled – I don't need any help"— then watch out!

People get very righteous about their ability to create their own path and that comes from a place of fear of being let down. They also often don't want to owe anybody else. Or they're so afraid of not being able to do it on their own that they have to prove to the world that they *can* do it all on their own.

If you say "I never find money," then you will never find money. Be open to finding it and it will show up. You're always provided for if you let it in. Some of the juiciest delicious shifts you'll get around who you are come from experiencing things along the journey of receiving.

Here's the thing: We all need each other. You can go your whole life kicking and screaming about how you got your stuff yourself, but the interesting thing of it is that we could all benefit from some assistance.

When you look at your history, likely, people were nudging you along at all the right times. We all bring unique gifts to the table and when we're in the mindset of "I've got this," the Universe has no place to bring it in for you. It's like the help from the Universe is just not welcome. How else might the Universe use the vehicle of other people on the planet to assist you?

Be open to more.

FREEDOM TIP #9:

The Universe writes your paycheck – it all comes from Source so if you've decided that's all you're going to get and that's all you deserve, then the Universe is not going to disappoint you --- if you decide "I don't need to know where it comes from, or know all the details, I just have to put my order in to the kitchen of the Universe," then it will present. It might not show up in your timing; it will be in Divine timing and it will arrive in any way you are open to receiving.

Be Grateful for What You Have

If abundance isn't coming your way, you've likely created some kind of belief around the idea that you have a hard time receiving. Like the famous Bob Newhart comedy skit of the same name, Stop it! Sometimes you just have to be over-the-moon grateful for what you *do* have, and forget about what you don't have yet. Some people reading this book may be living in a car or couch surfing but, for whatever reason, that condition is assisting them on their journey. Whatever is happening for you, right now, embrace it and let go of the fear. Maybe you're living in your car because you'll be able to help someone down the road who is also living in their car. You don't really know, you don't always see all of it, but you are always looked after and these are all simply experiences to catapult you forward into your own amazingness.

Write down a list of what you have – do you have food in your pantry? Clothes in your cupboard? Are you breathing? Do you have a vehicle, a place to sleep, a home? Be grateful, because that's a prime way of bringing to you more things for which to be grateful.

When you're in a place of worry and fear, you are bringing more of those things to you – whatever you're worrying about is like praying for what you don't want.

Some people are thinking "Yeah, right, that's easier said than done." They're absolutely correct. Shifting your focus like that takes practice. However, whatever you're focusing on will expand. Even just a blade of grass – how beautiful is that?

Wherever you are, you'll find something beautiful and focus your energy on that. Look in the mirror – there's something beautiful staring right back at you.

Everybody has something about them, their physical being, that they love – maybe it's your eyes, lips, nose, or skin. Focus on that and be grateful for that, and everything will start to shift.

Abundance

So, there are a few things to remember when allowing your abundance to find you.

First of all, it's important to be willing to receive. It's also important to let go of any judgement you might have around where that abundance is coming from...and ask for assistance. All of this brings up the issue of limiting beliefs.

Our beliefs are created by logic and our ego, and these both stem from our thoughts. People say that our thoughts, which come from our logical mind and our ego, create our reality. They often limit us: positive self-talk can assist in shifting the vibration we are emanating out, and that's good because how we feel is more important than what we are thinking.

The idea is to tap in to the deep knowing of your being, your genetics, your DNA, that deep knowing that says we're all created from stardust; we're all of the One; we are here to have our own experiences.

It is your own birthright to have everything you desire, and that is the difference between desire and need. The guilt you feel when you receive has nothing to do with "you." That comes from old beliefs, or judgements of others that came through when they received something.

Guilt around receiving comes from fear and lack, and feeling unworthy. Some people choose to have more perceptively interesting experiences than others, but we're all human and we're all made from the same stardust. A lot of people believe in the power of affirmations, but these affirmations should make you feel brighter and lighter in order to provide value.

FREEDOM TIP # 10:

Create space for the Universe to deliver what is yours by divine birth right. Sit in a different chair at dinner each night; take a different route to work or school each day; use your computer mouse with the "wrong" hand; brush your teeth with your other hand. You can likely come up with some interesting ideas yourself. There's no place for routine and expectation in the flow.

Tithing

Do you tip with the intention of getting it back tenfold?

Do you tip from a place of lack? I.e. do you ever find yourself saying, "I wish I could give you more... I just can't right now."

Do you count your pennies and then say: "No I can't do this?" Or do you say YES to what presents and let the Universe figure out how to bring it all together? Do you set intentions, take action and know it is all coming together without the need to know how?

Part of all this is about tithing and letting go of the expectation that something will come back to you tenfold. It's about feeling grateful and tapping into the knowledge that you have more than enough. So much that you can share.

Remember the "Or Better"

What do you want? Write it down and add the words, "OR BETTER" at the end.

At one point in my life I was a single mom with two kids and I was struggling to make ends meet. I had said to the Universe that I wanted $30,000 in unexpected income in the next 30 days or better. And I decided that that money could come in from anywhere.

One day I was at work and the receptionist came running upstairs to my office. "Call the radio station!" she hollered. "Why?" I asked "You won something!" That "something" turned out to be double my last paycheque plus tickets to a Brad Paisley concert.

The next week I was told that my services were no longer required at the company I was working for. I was in sales and I had done my job amazingly well. "We can't keep up," my boss said. "We can't expand that quickly and we're not sure if we want to expand that much."

Somehow, I had to find the energy to believe that this was all happening *for* me, and not *to* me.

But now I was out of a job and normally I didn't get paid my commission on the orders I had generated until those orders were complete. My boss coached me a little on what to do and I went in to a meeting with the owner of the company.

In the end, I received $11,000 for my final paycheque and the $5,000 from the radio station. While all this was playing out my grandmother gave me a cheque for $25,000 because she had decided to do a living will and this was my share. Total within 30 days of asking: $41,000. The "or better" had truly shown up. That was validation for me that this stuff works.

FREEDOM TIP #11:

When you're visualizing, or when you're saying affirmations, make sure it is believable for you. Picture yourself with whatever it is you want to manifest and feel the emotions as if it has already happened. Remember it will be in divine timing as things come up to assist you in becoming the vibration to match your request.

Give and Receive Equally

Here's something else that worked for me: When I give something to somebody I do it with no strings attached. I receive the most amazing feeling of love and gratitude just through the act of being of love and assistance to someone. Other people want to feel good, too. So, who am I to take that wonderful feeling of generosity away from them? In receiving gracefully what someone else offers me, I'm allowing them to feel suffused with love and gratitude as well. Everyone wins.

If you give in gratitude and receive willingly often enough, it becomes your normal. It's not spectacular anymore, it just is. It's like the first time you connect with nature: I remember being on a trail walking somewhere with my dogs and I felt overcome by the beauty and awe of the place. I could feel the blueberry bushes, the water, the eagle circling in the sky overhead, the mountains. I was experiencing all of it on every level with every single cell in my body and it was off-the-charts orgasmic.

The next time I went out walking, the appreciation was the same, but the surprise of it all was gone. The awesomeness had become my new normal. It works that way with other aspects of abundance, as well.

And that's how it should be. We have one of the most spectacular playgrounds in the Universe.

Here's a Tip:

I have a trick that I use to keep myself on track and I've taught this to my kids as well. The Universe will not recognise the words "don't," "won't," "can't," "haven't," etc., so you would be well advised to avoid using them. Here is an example: my daughter was going to a track meet and she kept saying "Mom I don't want it to rain!" I reminded her that the Universe doesn't hear the word "don't" and it was no doubt hearing "I want it to rain!" Kylee promptly changed her statement to "I want a dry track for my race." You see: she changed her vibration to what she wanted instead of what she was hoping to avoid. It's a subtle shift and a big one. By the way, the track was dry for her race and then right afterwards there was a massive downpour of rain.

Chapter Four: Everything is Happening For You

Shift your perspective and experience the joy of being guided to what's in the highest for you in the moment.

Kaayla Vedder

Sometimes you can say things to people in the most loving way, speaking your truth for the betterment of all... and the response can stun you.

People run things through filters of shame, guilt, not being enough, and so much more and, as they share their version of a story, they will be seeking to validate that they are right. The thing is, there is no right or wrong.

When the Universe presents an opportunity through a conversation, and you feel that you have to defend yourself, it is simply providing you an opportunity to release some limiting beliefs about yourself. You can choose to say "thank you" to the Universe or defend yourself.

The point to remember is that you are only responsible for yourself and your intentions. You have no control over how others receive information. Listening with a loving, neutral ear takes the power away from the story.

None of what we're feeling has anything to do with anyone else, in fact. *You* get to decide how you are feeling, not anyone else. We are all here triggering each other to release and experience feelings that have been buried way down deep. And *liberation* can only come from allowing yourself to experience these feelings without having to attach a story to them.

When we stop and examine the emotions that are coming up to go, things can slow down and get really yucky. Find a way to trust in the Universe and know that you are being totally looked after. You are safe, you're not broken and you don't need to be fixed; everything is happening *for* you and not *to* you. Breathe...

Just about anything can trigger us. The reason for the trigger isn't important...who cares why these things happen? Your ego is just using the information to try to keep you where you are, distracting your brain with a perceived need to know.

Things are much simpler when you can just see that everyone is on a journey of awakening, and each journey is unique. The Universe is looking after everyone else just as much as it is looking after you. How boring would it be if we all had the same journey? When you can be neutral, and see that people are doing the best they can with what they know, you can reduce your anxiety around their welfare and relax into being more "you." It's not up to you to assist people in any way, unless they ask. Even then they will get what they require as they require it. They may never fully understand you or your journey, and that's OK. You don't have to defend yourself or convince anybody of anything. Because things are happening *for* you, not *to* you.

58

Surrendering to What Presents

We tend to attach ourselves to unimportant details and try to understand situations in our lives with logical minds. The real key to a happy life is surrendering to what presents. That's how the Universe serves us, providing us with whatever is in our highest, even though it doesn't perceptively seem like it.

Life's magic reaches us through all of the little coincidences and happy accidents we encounter. Social science says that we think 60,000 thoughts a day and we know that some of these thoughts involve putting our order in to the Universe. A lot of things have to happen so that order can be filled, and a lot of people around the world may have to do certain things to make it all come about. Sometimes that takes more time than we would like, and sometimes it doesn't look as though what we want is coming through for us. That would be the "or better" shining through.

Just trust that things are happening exactly as they should and keep your thoughts on the final result.

If you change your mind about what you want, or feel self-doubt and worry taking over, you run the risk of confusing the Universe.

You are manifesting your life, you are the Universe, you are the gift, you get to create your plan. You just need to have an idea of where you want yourself to go, then move some energy on the subject and see if it grows legs. Remember, things will come up along the way to assist you in releasing thoughts and feelings that keep you from being a vibrational match for what you want.

The Universe will take care of the rest.

59

Leonard Cohen once said "There's a crack in everything — that's how the light gets in." You don't know the "how," which doesn't mean the dream is not being delivered. It *is* being delivered.

When we strive for perfection from other people — or anything in life, for that matter — the energy we bring to the project keeps us from our end result because the Divine always knows the fastest, quickest, most delicious way to get you to the end result.

But if you're trying to get involved so you can make the situation perfect, you're going to slow it down.

When we are used to being perceptively in control, and knowing every moment of every plan, it can be very unfamiliar to enter into flow and trust in the unseen plan that the Universe has for you.

Knowing "everything" becomes a place of safety.

When you're in flow, you release the need to know what's next. Flow is about embracing the "not knowing," and trusting that the Universe has your back.

Why not consider giving up attempting to control all the details of how this romance is going to happen, and surrender to the flow.

Take the car out of park and just put it in gear and drive. You'll get where you want to go.

It doesn't matter which way you turn, you can't get it wrong, because everything is happening *for* you, not *to* you.

And sometimes that's a huge surprise.

FREEDOM TIP#12:

Most of the things people believe are facts are simply opinions or beliefs. It takes courage to see beyond the obvious and step into the uncharted territories of being the first to attempt something, or to simply believe that anything is possible, and be open to the "or better."

My New Massage Table

Here's an example: One day I mentioned to my husband that I kept getting the feeling that I should get a massage table. This was weird. I didn't need one and I wasn't planning to set up a business of any sort. So, I shrugged it off and moved on with my life.

A couple of weeks later my mom took a fall and severely broke her ankle. She called me to come and help her, and together we called an ambulance.

In due course, she was admitted to the hospital and told she had to wait for surgery. She was going to require some pins and plates in her ankle, and she was going to be out of commission for at least six weeks.

My mom has her own energy work business doing a variety of things — reiki, reflexology, shiatsu, etc.

She asked me to call her clients and to postpone all of her appointments until she could be back to work.

So, I'm calling all these people and this one guy says, "Well, what do you do?"

"What makes you think I do anything?" I asked.

"I just have this feeling," he said.

61

"I don't do anything like my mom does," I said. "I don't actually touch people in the work I do." I was doing everything I could to discourage this man. Then I said: "You don't have to come in to see me, I can work on you quantumly. I simply tune in to your higher levels and move the energy that is interfering with whatever is in the highest for you."

"Do you have any openings tomorrow?" he asked.

"I don't know," I said. "I don't have my schedule with me right now — I am at my mom's place."

I got off the phone with him and I was standing back thinking, "What the hell just happened there? I don't have a schedule, and I don't do sessions for anyone other than family and friends."

It was like something just took over and this guy was not going to take no for an answer.

This was just hilarious because I came home and before I could even tell my husband what had happened he said, "your massage table came for you today." He had gone ahead and ordered the table as a surprise gift! When it had arrived, he had set it up in the spare room.

I shared with my husband and daughter what had happened that afternoon and my daughter, Cassidy, said to me "Mom, I don't get why you are so nervous, just do what you do."

I phoned the guy back and when he didn't answer, I left a message. I thought, "Phew, I don't have to do this, it's Friday evening and he didn't answer."

But within 30 minutes, he called back, and I booked him in for first thing the next morning. I was nervous and excited: this was my first appointment with someone from outside of my direct circle.

The appointment went well, and he booked many more appointments and told people about the sessions; then more clients came. It was what presented.

Then, more and more clients started coming, and then one of my clients said to me "you should do a meditation night where people could get together as a group."

She hosted a meditation night at her place and, lo and behold, meditation clearing nights were born.

When my mother broke her ankle, I could never have predicted that it would result in me building up a business and holding meditation nights.

Although I had a general sense that I wanted to be of service and contribution in the world, I didn't have a roadmap that set out where I wanted to go. But it was definitely something that happened *for* me, not *to* me.

FREEDOM TIP # 13:

As painful as it may be at times in your life, see everything from above the density and trust that the Universe has your back. Take a breath and recognize you are being guided to what is in the highest for everyone.

You Are Amazing!

Everything — and I mean *everything!* — that is brought to you is happening for you, assisting you and catapulting you into your own amazingness, the clearest and brightest experience of what you really are, what you agreed to be before you came into this body for all of these experiences.

Your higher self set it all up. Everything in the universe is forward and out. Are you here to learn lessons with your logical mind?

Or are you here to experience things to assist you in remembering how amazing you truly are?

Are you a creator, creating opportunities to experience more of your own brilliance and amazingness?

We are all perfect in our imperfections. WE are LOVE! WE are Creator! WE are the Universe! Come up, way up above the density of it all, and see the love. Let's make no apologies for who I am or who you are; no judgements and no forgiveness are required!

Do you get it? Do you really get it? You are freaking amazing! Brilliant! Divine! I love you so much! You are the creator, the inventor, the director, producer, actor and audience of it all. You are the giver. **YOU ARE THE GIFT!**

Chapter Five: Be Who You're Meant to Be

"I am seeking. I am striving. I am in it with all my heart."

- Vincent van Gogh

Many of us are extremely compassionate with others, but it's a different story entirely when it comes to how we treat ourselves.

We know we're supposed to be OK with who we are, and we know that compassion for others is supposed to start with compassion for ourselves.

So, we say that we love ourselves, and we try to believe it's true... and then we proceed to criticize ourselves for a whole list of perceived shortcomings and failings. Our self-talk becomes destructive; we begin to judge everything we do.

Do you realize that you are not the "identities," you assume? You're not The Perfect Mom, The Best-Loved Teacher, The Successful Boss, The Brilliant Scientist, The Amazing Wife. You probably like some of these identities, and there are some you probably wish you didn't have.

The trick is to dance in and out of all of them without fear or resistance or competition.

Remember that you don't have to live up to the illusions that each of those identities (and others) suggest are desirable.

You are perfect in your own way, exactly as the Divine child of God you came here to be. So, stop worrying about what others think of you. That's none of your business! It is your business to be concerned with what YOU think of you! You are so loved! You have purpose and you matter!

Be Authentic

I am so grateful for the people and clients I have attracted into my life. I had a wonderful conversation recently with an amazing "soul sista." We talked about being our authentic selves, letting all of the identities we've assumed just drop and then getting down to the business of being who we truly are.

I have had many teachers and mentors on my journey and I remember thinking, "Man, I would love to be as gentle, kind, sweet and loving as they are, and just be content with the air around me like they are." I tried numerous times to reach this unrealistic goal of being like others, and eventually it came time to be who I truly am.

I had to become comfortable with stepping into who I am and how I shine my light. I may not be all soft and gentle like some of my mentors, however who I am is coming from a place of total love and compassion...and it comes with my own authentic spin. Respecting and honouring everyone — including myself — for where we are on our journey is critically important to our wellbeing.

It is easy to fall into the habit of being who you think people want you to be, and to do things the way you are told to do things. Seriously, though, how boring would the world be without our individuality?

We can all relate to having to behave a certain way for specific situations. Like, when you go to school or work, you behave a certain way and sometimes there's a benefit to doing that.

But it's even more important to be your true authentic self and stand in your own light and let it shine. If people don't like it, then they probably aren't an energetic match for you. Be brave, be who you are!

Sometimes, when you are who you're truly meant to be, others' vibrations will shift as well, and by you being all of who you are, you assist others to do the same. You are so loved! You matter! You are more than enough!

FREEDOM TIP #14:

Get a piece of paper and draw a line down the centre, creating two columns. Write "Identities I Love "at the top of one column and write "Identities I Could Do Without" at the top of the other column. Write as many identities as you can in each column. When you're done, recognize without judgment how you can dance in and out of all of these identities without competition or attachment.

Fitting In

Have you ever felt like you just don't fit in? Have you ever looked at the people in your life and thought "they just don't get me, nobody really knows me"? Have you spent time trying to do what is expected of you and still feel like it's not authentic?

Think way back as far as you can, to a time when you felt at peace. Maybe you can't remember, and that's OK, it will come back to you. If you can remember that time of peace, then I invite you to use your imagination and connect back to that place, feel the energy of how amazing you are, with all your own unique gifts.

As much as I would love to be able to say that I have always been 100% comfortable with being my authentic self, that is definitely not the way things have always been for me.

I was born different, for sure, and I've always known that I marched to a different drummer, which has been fine with me.

But I've spent an awful lot of my life struggling to find a way to figure out who I am and express it fearlessly and enthusiastically. And nowhere has this been a more fascinating journey than in the area of my romantic relationships.

I've had some interesting relationships. May I share a little bit of that?

Whenever I've been in a relationship, I've thought I truly loved the man I've been with and, truly, they've all had some great qualities that I initially found very attractive.

But there came a point in each case where I came to realize that I was headed for a much bigger heartbreak if we didn't break up. I've come to trust that, for whatever reason, I'm being looked after, even if in that moment it doesn't seem like it.

I married my first husband when I was 19 years old and if I had listened to what was presenting before saying, "I do," I would have saved us both a lot of grief.

But I was young and headstrong and I was determined to marry this young man in order to overcome the fear of being alone that struck me whenever we talked about breaking up.

But it was never going to work.

We had some areas of massive misalignment, especially in the area of spirituality, and I eventually realized that in order to live an authentic life myself, I had to leave the marriage. It was a hard thing to do. And it was the right thing for me to do.

After that marriage ended I had a couple of long-term relationships with wonderful men with whom I shared a love of adventure and some great travelling experiences.

The first man found a woman, who he thought, for a while, was a better match for him. After leaving me for some months he arrived back in my driveway one day asking to be taken back. The answer was a clear "No." For me to stand in the authentic truth of who I was, I knew I couldn't resume our relationship. Much as I cared about him.

The other man and I had a glorious relationship for a while but we split up when the subject of children came up: I had told him about the many surgeries I had had in the past, and that my chances of pregnancy were slim-to-none; I felt that, if there were possibly a way, I would love to become a mother.

But he absolutely didn't want any kids and, again, for me to stand in the truth of who I am, I absolutely had to make sure that I didn't settle for less life than I thought I was seeking.

And so, life went on and eventually I met the man who was to become my second husband.

At the beginning of our relationship I thought it was really sweet that he would call me to make sure I got home from work safely.

He had a big house and I was there all the time anyway, but we didn't share a deep, passionate, loving connection.

As time went on, it became clear that what we did share was a house. I moved in with him and shortly thereafter I was scheduled for an operation to remove yet another ovarian cyst. I found out that I was pregnant and it was such a shock – nothing else in the whole world mattered! When my partner asked me to marry him, I wondered if he even loved me.

I was more afraid of being a single mom than I was of being in a loveless marriage, however. It took me a long time to realize that he actually did love me, in fact he loved me as much as he could love anybody.

But the situation was less than ideal, and his family and I didn't get along well. Maybe you can relate? As Bishop T.D. Jakes puts it, our "love tanks" were different sizes.

"There are people amongst us. Like you and like me, and many people in this room, who are voluminous. We are 10-gallon people. But we may have been born into families of people that have pint capacity."

- Bishop T.D. Jakes

Have you ever been dating someone and felt that little thrill of excitement you get when they call you to make sure you made it home OK? Then they text you to see how your day is going throughout the day.

It seems so sweet and endearing that someone cares so much about you that they are checking on you to make sure you're alright.

Have you ever been with a person who is so jovial and outgoing when others are around, or they come across as sweet and kind, and your friends and family think they are funny and approachable? What happens when there is no one around? Do they talk badly about other people? Does it sometimes seem like they are boasting about themselves?

What if they are really private — maybe they don't want the blinds open because someone might look inside at their life? What if, when you go to hang out with your friends, they say, "I really wish you would stay home. I want to spend time with you. I love you." And if you go, they make you feel guilty for going.

What if you just can't seem to get it right, no matter what you do ? What if, when you go to work and come home, your partner doesn't believe you have been at work? What if they think you have been out with another romantic partner? What if they simply don't trust you or believe anything you say?

What if they put your children at risk to prove that the fantasy in their head is real (when it's not). Do you find yourself arguing with them about the smallest things? If you said the sky is blue would they say "No, it's orange"?

What if, every time you are planning to order food in, you get the order all figured out... but for some reason they always change the plan and order something else, or nothing at all?

What if, over a long, time-consuming process, you find yourself worn out with the effort of defending your appearance, your opinions and your beliefs. And it's just not worth sharing your opinion or point of view anymore because your partner simply belittles you or gets angry?

Defending yourself against the constant barrage of reasons why you're insufficient in every way is exhausting.

What if you just get so tired you start to think that maybe they're right? What if you start to think that you are not enough, that you're unattractive, lazy or unimportant? What if, over time, your family and friends stop coming around because they can feel the tension?

What if you wake up one day simply drained from the effort of having to walk on egg shells all the time? What if you think to yourself, "Oh my God, I am so stupid for being in this situation. How did I get here?"

You're not alone. Many people experience unhealthy relationships. I have clients who have come out the other end and I have clients who have stayed.

The great thing is, you can choose whether to stay or go. Sometimes it seems easier to stay simply because the situation is predictable and there is comfort in knowing how you are supposed to behave.

I myself had a "choice point moment" one Christmas at a neighbour's party. I was sitting in a big red comfy chair drinking a glass of wine and smoking a minty cigarette. I began to think about my relationship and realized I had been here before.

For the past four years I'd been going to this same Christmas party, sat in this same chair and visited these same people and questioned my life and my relationship. I'd been going alone to marriage counselling for almost a year by then. And I realized things weren't going to change. So I had to either accept things as they were, or make a change. I opted to make a change.

We create the world we experience each and every day. When we change/heal the way we think and feel about ourselves, we change/heal the entire Universe.

You may think you are simply a small little bit in a big Universe; however you are a powerful creator.

It is fractally impossible not to assist all of humanity when you assist yourself. You are so loved! You Matter! You are more than enough!

You are Creator.

Truth is not something you think about, it's something you feel. It comes from your heart as a knowing, and it arrives without the assistance of your brain, or your ego.

When you are looking for your own guidance and direction, tap into your heart to find the truth.

FREEDOM TIP #15:

Ask! Ask each day of any of your guides, angels and higher levels. Ask them to show you what you need to know to be the beautiful shining light that you know you are.

There is no room for the logical mind in this process; it will actually slow you down.

But your logical mind can only know what has been, what once was. That is not a template for an unknown future.

Your mind will want to dissect the world around you and understand it. It wants to keep everything in a certain order to provide explanations and then lay blame.

Your heart gives you the direction in which you would be well advised to head. You are an infinite being of light having an experience in a human body.

Your higher levels (which are a part of you) have conspired to generate all the events of your life occur in order to propel you forward into your own knowing.

Let your heart's knowledge point you in the direction that is in the highest for you.

Never allow another to define you. You have your own truth. Simply embrace it.

FREEDOM TIP #16:

From the moment we are born, we are being taught how to relate and respond to everything around us. We are taught from our parents and siblings, who have been taught from all the adults in their lives, and so on…these adults have passed down all the things they have been taught. It is actually outdated information. It contains countless limiting beliefs. So here we go on this journey of remembering before we were taught to forget. Open your mind and your body to experience the remembering. You are not wrong.

Chapter Six: Create a Drama-Free Zone

So many people prefer to live in drama because it's comfortable. It's like someone staying in a bad marriage or relationship - it's easier to stay because they know what to expect every day, versus leaving and not knowing what to expect.

*- **Ellen DeGeneres***

I live a dramatic life, it's just not on TV yet.

*- **Marc Wallice***

I may not lead the most dramatic life, but in my brain, it's 'War and Peace' everyday.

*- **Rufus Wainwright***

Many of us can lay the blame for some of the struggles we've had straight at the feet of our parents.

We think that if they had been somehow more ideal as people and as parents, we would have had an easier ride. We wouldn't have had to deal with quite so much drama in our world.

What do parents do wrong? Check the list.

As an adult child, you might feel that your parents were/are:

- hypercritical
- absent
- alcoholic
- unloving
- distant
- perfectionist
- lax
- irresponsible
- controlling
- superficial
- demanding
- and more

At some point, you might have thought, "What was my mom/dad thinking when they _____?" The answer is that they probably weren't thinking at all. At least, they weren't thinking about hurting you. Just like you, a lot of their behaviour was driven by subconscious prompts implanted in their brains by their own parents. Their parents also did the same thing, so they've been carrying their parents' stuff, who were carrying their parents' stuff who were...you get the picture. Now you're carrying everybody's stuff, going back for countless generations.

The other part of it is that when we judge people or people judge us, or there's any kind of trauma, or upset happening in our lives, we can "give away" aspects of ourselves. This allows us to fit in, pass muster, earn approval or otherwise win points.

To fit in, we might give away parts of our sense of humour that other people found brash. We might give away vulnerable behaviour that other people found "soft."

We also might give away our sense of groundedness that other people thought was boring, or joyfulness that other people found irritating. These little pieces of ourselves get scattered all over the place, out in the Universe and deep down inside us. It's a bit messy.

And, just like a computer, we need to be defragged every now and then, so we can release the crap we came into this world wearing, and the crap we picked up along the way.

We need to shake the energy off, kind of a like a dog that shakes when it stands up. We need to move the energy.

Animals are great teachers, by the way. An animal in the wild doesn't live his or her life constantly thinking "When am I going to die?"

Instead, animals are solidly in the moment. When something traumatic happens to an animal in the wild, then and only then do they kick into "fight, flight or freeze" mode. They don't spend their lives wrapped up in drama, waiting for the other shoe to fall. But when it happens and it's over, then they shake it off.

I invite you to practise staying in the moment, too.

Allow yourself to experience that connection with the moment. That's how you open your heart, you simply allow yourself to experience your emotions without having to connect a story to them.

Somewhere along the way we've been taught not to do that – it's a thing people have decided is a weakness, and it's not.

If we can release all of that judgement and then allow ourselves to experience it, whatever "it" is, we liberate ourselves and companions.

The Truth about Your Stories

Everything you have experienced deeply has propelled you forward farther and faster – especially the juicy and delicious things that have gone perceptively wrong.

The perceptively worse the experience, the farther you have been propelled forward into a place of divine, unconditional love.

A lot of people I know, myself included, have a theory that before we are even born, our souls make certain agreements about what we are going to experience in our next lifetime.

We agree to play a role in specific kinds of stories. But those are just stories. You are not the story or the drama.

You are a beautiful being of light; your vehicle is your physical body, you are here to experience this beautiful heaven on Earth, to wake up to all that you are, and reconnect with the true essence of you. When you can set the drama aside, stand in your light and simply choose love, you are assisting all of humanity.

Let Go of What You Think It Should Look Like

People are funny. We have an idea of what it looks like to be lovable, or acceptable, or successful.

There's a whole energy within humanity that's decided that if you have a big house and a car and, and, and, and…whatever, then you deserve to be loved.

Nonsense!

Far better to be open to whatever your condition is in life, and look at what you have with gratitude and love. You could be a homeless person sleeping in a park under a tree, and the gratitude for that tree could be immense. It may not be perceptively "desirable" when measured against all the goodies you could be yearning to enjoy. But in that moment, in that gratitude you can suspend your dissatisfaction around any perceptively undesirable conditions you are facing.

And the rest of us would be well served to stay out of judgement.

Maybe the person who is sleeping under the tree agreed to come here for that experience. It doesn't mean that the wealthy person's journey is any easier than the person sleeping under the tree.

They are just different experiences.

The wealthy person might declare bankruptcy or the homeless person might win a million dollars. Whatever it is, being in the flow of whatever your journey is — whether you perceive it as good or bad — allows you to surrender to the joy you can experience moment by moment by moment. Whatever that is at the time. Without fuss. Without drama.

All of those experiences are what create your journey. Just let go of what other people claim your journey is supposed to look like. Relinquish the need for drama. Accept each moment as it comes. And let go of the judgement of what you're experiencing.

We are spiritual beings having human experiences. Our spirits are complete and whole and do not need fixing. Our physical bodies, including our minds, are guiding us towards awakening or "healing" as Mass Consciousness likes to call it.

So, when a client comes in to see me with aches and pains or some sort of injury, illness or disease, it is simply an opportunity to witness density being removed in order to allow the spirit to awaken. And with that as our context, of what use is drama?

Divinity and Religion

When I was very young, I remember asking people a lot of questions about religion, and not getting answers that made sense to me.

My first husband was a very committed Jehovah's Witness and in that religion at the time, you had to study before you could get baptized. There were a lot of other rules as well that I felt served only to restrict our access to the Divine. It seemed very hypocritical to me, and I never bought into all that.

In fact, it struck me that all of these rules around religion actually served to create more drama in our lives, rather than less. They made people measure themselves against arbitrary standards of goodness or purity or holiness, and of course, most of us can't measure up consistently to the benchmark. So we see ourselves as lacking, and that is stressful.

It also alienates us from our Creator: If we have to follow all those complicated rules in order to gain His/Her approval, or even just our Creator's acceptance, then why bother trying? We'll never be good enough.

It's almost as though the fear of not being good enough or holy enough creates a mechanism by which people can be controlled.

Way back in the day, people who were considered witches were burned at the stake simply because most of humanity was taught to believe that all witches were evil and scary and they worked against God.

Even Jesus was crucified because his teachings did not align with the standard religious rules of his day. He was executed for being different. We are all created of the same stardust. We are all connected to the Divine. Does anything else really matter?

I think that although many religious organizations do a lot of good in the world, they are very hierarchical.

The rules are not essentially spirit-related, they are logical, procedural and structural. They come from ego and they relate to the balance of power in the world. Power has a big impact on drama.

The energetic belief system that I embrace, by contrast, has no room for logic: it slows you down.

I believe that in acknowledging our individual connection to the Divine, and honouring the Divine within our hearts, we can follow the guidance that is laid before us to live out the joy that is available to us as spiritual beings having a human experience.

The more you trust that the Universe has your back and you are completely looked after, and the more you believe it, the more easily you can release all of your fears, whether they were handed down to you from a parent or a boss or whoever. We're never given more than we can handle, we never experience anything that doesn't assist us, even things that are perceptively uncomfortable, like lack of money.

Things don't always look like we thought they were going to look. And the more we lean into that way of being, the less drama we perceptively create for ourselves.

Chapter Seven: Your Heart-Centred Power

"Our friends, our lovers, our spouses, even our children are not ours; they belong only to themselves. Possessive and controlling friendships and relationships can be as harmful as neglect, a powerful truth about the importance of letting go. It has guided me in both my private and professional life ever since. I have often quoted it as an excellent model for parenthood, which is a gradual, wonderful - and sometimes painful - process of letting go. It begins with the cutting of the umbilical cord and ends when you hand over the keys of your car. They will fly the nest, but if you freely and willingly let them go then they will always come back."

- Alison Willcocks

If you love something, set it free. If it comes back to you, it's yours. If it doesn't, it never was. We do not possess anything in this world, least of all other people. We only imagine that we do.

- Alison Willcocks

You are the giver, you are the gift

- Anonymous

I took a group to a tiny little town tucked up against the Sangre de Cristo Mountains in Colorado last year, where I had the pleasure and honour of facilitating an amazing Awakening Retreat.

It was a very busy trip and there wasn't a lot of down time because it really wasn't a vacation. Most of the members of the group hadn't known what they were getting into, and there was huge resistance around the pace we kept up. Part of the program I laid out for the group was based upon the fact that when your physical body experiences a state of feeling "tired," your mental body is unable to resist what happens to you, and beautiful things start to occur. The ego falls away, and it is so much easier to receive activations and upgrades. The density and limiting beliefs come up in your face.

Part of my journey on this retreat was around learning to accept the fact that I would be a trigger for people. The exercises I led would put me in the position of participants' mothers, teachers, rule makers and others who, in the past, had helped participants generate a state of unhappiness. My role, whether conscious or not, was to trigger deep-seated emotions that, once in the open, could be dealt with and relinquished. We call this "coming up to go." The cool thing is that you can look at what comes up for you, however or whenever it comes up. ***Whatever you're feeling is never about the other person;*** it's always your own stuff, and setting it free is a cause for celebration.

Let me explain a little more: triggers occur when you're just being your sweet innocent self, coming from a place of purity and love, and doing your thing. Suddenly someone gets up in your face and flips their stuff at you. When that happens, it brings up a lot of density. You might be tempted to react and flip your stuff back at them. You get upset, they get upset and everyone's feeling defiant and hurt. We've got victims, we've got persecutors and we've got a whole lot of misery.

One or both of you may try to recruit others to jump on your band wagon so you can prove how wrong the other guy is. We all want validation, right? Everybody is just trying to keep themselves safe. Everybody's ego is having a field day.

In a perfect world, everybody takes a look at what triggered them, and tries to resolve the age-old hurt at the bottom of it so they understand it's an old pattern, and to let it go. At least, the opportunity to do that is there. Whether we take advantage of it is another issue.

FREEDOM TIP #17:

You don't have to examine an issue when you feel triggered; you can simply acknowledge the emotion without having to connect a story to it. Just say "Thank you!" to the Universe for showing you that there is something left to go. Allow yourself to experience the emotions that you denied yourself, either when the event first occurred or now, with or without the story that goes along with it. If it all sucked, then let it suck! Then, let it, and the story, go.

During the retreat I led, the Universe brought everything up for everyone perfectly. We had many plans that we had held very loosely, and these plans changed daily, based on what else was presenting (the "Or Better!").

The thing to remember is that you can be a trigger without doing anything at all. It's not about being malicious, vindictive, manipulative, wanting to push people's buttons or anything like that – you can trigger people when you're just being you.

85

When your vibration is much higher than someone else's, and their vibration is coming up to meet yours, the whole process can create resistance and a state of discomfort. When this happens, it means that the Universe is giving you beautiful opportunities to look at what you're holding onto in order to keep yourself perceptively safe. The approach gives you the opportunity to truly stand in who you are in authenticity and integrity, trusting that the Universe has your back. I was shown many entanglements and manipulations on that trip, as well as energies and entities that had to shift. I was consistently being called to witness and assist in moving energy. It was an honour to be of such service, to watch as things moved, willingly or not. It was inspiring to see the members of my group being courageous enough to be totally honest with themselves. This may not be comfortable for people, as it's unfamiliar. When you let yourself be in that space, it's incredibly enlightenng, and .that's where Divine Grace comes in.

Right Here, Right Now

All you've got is right here, right now. The future isn't here yet so there's no point trying to deal with it right now. Whatever's going to happen will happen regardless of how much you worry about it now, or try to change it. It's going to be what it's going to be. And all that effort you put into trying to control it or revise it, all that energy you expended, doesn't change what it's going to be. It's the same thing with your awakening journey: the results arrive in perfect timing, never in *our* timing, and they may not look like everyone else's results. Thank God! How boring would it be if we all looked the same an had the same superpowers?

86

True Freedom is about participating in your own journey. Release those you have been carrying. Release the idea that you know, better than anybody, what's best for other people, and release those people, too. Find the way that is best for you. Practise with some of the activities in this book and play with the energy. If you would like more concentrated assistance, contact me!

Be the leader that you came here to be! Wake up! You are so loved! You matter! You are more than enough! Stand in your own heart-centred power and be who you came here to be.

I had a client who was putting a lot of energy and action into getting a new position within the company for which she worked. She was doing her best to make this happen, and she put a lot of focus on what she had decided would be the best fit for her. The Universe had a much better idea. While she was taking action, and putting her focus on the position she really wanted, she was feeling extremely unhappy with her current job.

You see, she was busy measuring what she thought she should be doing, and where she thought she should be in her career, based on where other people were, or where her family and friends thought she should be. The thing is, you really can't get it wrong. The Universe is always guiding you in the direction that is in the highest for you. It's when you resist the guidance, and judge it, or compare yourself to others, that you really miss the good stuff. My client didn't get the job she wanted.

But she did get the opportunity to take a look at her existing job and, when she wasn't using other people's yardsticks, she came to realize that it actually was perfect for her. It allowed her to step into some skills, strengths and abilities that were unique to her. The great thing is that you can figure all this out in this life time, and go with the flow, or you can go kicking and screaming and get it in another life time. Either way, you will get it.

Divine Love

We are all amazing beings of light who are here to fly forward. (F.L.Y. = Fully Love Yourself.) We're here to love ourselves and love others. There's a whole cheering squad working behind the scenes on our behalf, loving us up and seeing how we've moved forward in our evolution. Our Higher Levels want us to tap into our amazingness and to do that we have to stop "guru-izing" other people. We have to be honest with ourselves, and check in to see if we're coming from a better than/less than place – there's no room for any of that in stepping into our amazingness.

FREEDOM TIP #18:

When you stand in your light, know, like you know, like you *know*, that nothing can touch you. Imagine a beautiful white light in the centre of your solar plexus. (This is just below your chest by your diaphragm) Take some nice deep belly breaths and imagine that light getting brighter and bigger with every breath, pulling air all the way down to your lower lungs, expanding your belly all the way out. The light is expanding through your entire body. With every breath, it expands out even farther, past your physical body until you are a beautiful blinding white light.

Chapter Eight: Changes Cha-Cha-Cha!

It is not the strongest of the species that survives, nor the most intelligent that survives. It is the one that is most adaptable to change.

- Charles Darwin

Making your unknown known is the important thing.

- Georgia O'Keeffe.

I love change. In fact, I have always loved change, I've always embraced it, and become excited about it. And when change is in the air, it gives me huge pleasure to reorganize a closet, and go on a cleansing rampage. When shift is happening, you have to get rid of the old to make room for the new. I'll clear out bags of items, reorganize, hang stuff up on new hangers, and rearrange drawers. There's something cathartic about it all that simply makes me feel light-hearted.

I love the excitement of the "not knowing" when change is underway. It's like having a Christmas present – you don't know what's in it but you love the fact that it's there. In fact, I actively court change by brushing my teeth with the wrong hand and I never sit at the same place at the kitchen table.

The thing for me is that I've always been comfortable with change – it's how I came in to this world, so I have an interesting time relating to people who are resistant to change. I see the resistance and I can comprehend it, but I have not experienced it.

Awakening to Wonders

There is a lot of change involved in this journey of awakening and, trust me, it's a journey that never ends. There is no real "destination." The journey just gets juicer and juicer.

How often have you personally experienced a moment of sudden understanding or enlightenment - then found yourself going back to what is familiar and comfortable?

You can go from feeling like you are really "getting it" to diving back into the need to understand. The logical mind has no place in this process of awakening.

The ego has too much to say and the mind actually slows you down. But as we become more comfortable with the process, we start to experience emotions of all kinds without judgement, and we simply relax into a state of feeling. It's amazing—colours get brighter, and you start to attract wonderful things magnetically. Then, somewhere along the way you start to analyze it all, or something triggers you, and you go back to what is familiar and predictable, even if it is perceptively creating unhappiness. Three steps forward....

This journey of awakening to blissful Divine love is available to you at all times. It's really about being completely honest with yourself. Completely naked, with no protective mechanisms, just you. It takes courage and practise to step into the unfamiliar and it takes practise to see things from above the density, and trust that, no matter what you do, you can't get it wrong. The things you once thought were spectacular and magnificent become your new normal.

It can sometimes feel like a bit of a Cha-Cha-Cha! when you are learning how to be in the flow of things.

It's so funny: I have clients who had no idea what it was like to connect back to themselves when they first started working with me. They didn't know what it was like to tap into their own beautiful light and simply shine.

They practised this awhile and found they were noticing things that were out of place, or they were being triggered and they began to question the entire process. This is completely normal and cause for celebration!

You see, there was a time when that very thing that you are questioning was a part of your "normal" and you didn't even see it before, much less examine it.

The things that come up along the way, things that happen with your family and friends — the drama, the story — are triggers You begin to feel less inclined to participate in them and more likely to take a neutral stand. Sometimes you simply recognize them as something you would like to move through quickly and easily; you're open to seeing what your part in the experience is, and you're willing to look after yourself, all the while loving the people in your life as they embark upon their own journey. The key is to detach yourself from any expectation of what things should look like or how they should play out. And do the "Changes Cha-Cha-Cha!"

Participation Is Key

To make this work for you, you have to jump in with both feet. Don't hold back. Isn't it funny

that as humans in this day and age we have become accustomed to instant gratification?

We want results right away and we want palpable results that we can see and measure and dissect.

Awakening is a process. It can take some time. But it's never too late to start an awakening journey and, to be totally honest, no matter who you are, your journey started way back before this lifetime, even if you were not consciously aware of having been on a journey until recently.

I encourage you to ask a lot of questions without necessarily needing to find any answers. You want to more or less tap yourself into the feeling that comes up from asking those questions. It takes energy, but it's not work. There are lots of people in this world who bip along with no cares and no worries. They like going to their job, and they like coming home to their family. But there's no fire in them and they don't seem to have a desire for something more. That's OK. There's nothing wrong with that. Those just aren't the people I'm here to serve. I'm here for the people who know there's something more and are willing to complete the activities that will help them uncover it.

When you come to feel that you're ready to have that potentially uncomfortable conversation, come and find me and we can continue your journey together.

FREEDOM TIP #19:

When you start to do the Cha-Cha, you also have the gift of becoming aware of the flow of the Universe. You begin to observe and trust in the flow. When you are in the flow, everything is easy and, even where there are things that are perceptively not so great, there is flow. When you are in Ego, everything is a struggle.

What Does That Look Like?

Lots of people want to move forward in their life. They want to go on their Awakening journey and manifest all kinds of wonderful things. They have dreams, dream charts, vision boards, positive affirmations and the like, and, when nothing happens, they're like, "Hey – this just isn't working. What's wrong?"

One of the things I do, is to help people remove some of the blocks that they have created to keep them the way they are. Let's say you're in your car and you want to go to your friend's new house. You have a result you want to achieve. You key the address to your GPS and away you go. You have no idea what roadblocks you are going to find on the way, or whether or not there will be detours, traffic accidents, weather problems or errant animals trying to cross the road in front of your vehicle. You're looking at this GPS and you just go for it, trusting that your GPS knows the easiest, fastest way to get you to your final destination. But here's the catch: *you have to take your car out of park.*

It almost doesn't matter which route you plan to follow, you absolutely have to start by getting in action.

When you shift into "drive," that's where the delicious stuff starts to show up: the serendipitous coincidences, the beautiful views along the way and the chance meeting with the person who is going to open the next door for you.

You have to take your car out of park, take some action, move some energy and be ready for the "Or Better." Sometimes, though, the detour doesn't look like it's leading to the "Or Better."

Divorce Wars: Change is Everywhere

It comes as no surprise to me that some of the clients I serve struggle with relationship issues. Living in an intimate partnership with another human being is one of the toughest things we humans set out to do on this planet. There can be a lot of conflict and our egos tend to get tangled up with one another in messy ways that don't contribute to our ultimate happiness.

Pulling the plug on a marriage or other kind of long-standing partnership is painful and emotional and there doesn't seem to be an easy fix to the challenges that go along with the aftermath of divorce. Other than to know that change is inevitable, and surrendering to change without judgement makes it all a lot easier. And although that part of the journey might not seem agreeable in any way, shape or form, it can, ultimately, lead to your "or better."

As I've mentioned before, my second marriage was OK until it wasn't. There were a lot of issues in the marriage and I felt very unhappy with the way we interacted. And my ex just couldn't bring himself to support my job.

I had a home-based business selling Party Lite candles and I would do a lot of public speaking in the line of duty. I was very much an inspirational speaker and my company would ask me to speak at large gatherings all over the place for this company.

My results and my leadership position within the company meant that I earned trips to Bermuda and other great spots. And along the way I had begun to remember that I had purpose and that I mattered in the world; I was OK and I had a lot to offer.

I invite anybody out there who suffers from low self-esteem to get involved in a home-based business. There are many of them from which to choose and many of these companies really do build participants' self-esteem. They bring in guest speakers and they have a lot of mentors on tap to help people become more of who they truly are. It can be life changing–and, in my case, Party Lite helped me get through the struggles of an unhappy marriage. The friends I made in the company helped show me that I had purpose and value. I assisted a lot of other women. And I started to think "What the heck – my husband doesn't have a nice word to say about any of this, even though he sees the money I'm bringing in. What's wrong with this picture?"

One day I was talking to another consultant in my company and I said, "You know, my business is just freaking booming – I have so many clients, there are so many consultants working with me, my bank account is full — this is just spectacular!"

The consultant said: "You know, the times in my life when my business has been that explosive are the times I've noticed that I'm not giving my relationship any attention."

And I said, "Oh."

My Friends Felt Unwelcome

I sat with that thought for a while. I didn't feel supported or loved. I felt sabotaged all the time, I felt small, and none of my family or friends wanted to come over to my house anymore because they felt unwelcome. There were a lot of other issues at play but the upshot was that, eventually, I left.

95

In the divorce, I just wanted what was fair. This was a big change for all of us and it was difficult to make the transition in some ways. But the "Or Better" eventually showed up for me, as it will for you if you are going through something similar. A lot of hurtful things can happen in a divorce. Sometimes one of the girls would refuse to go to her dad's and that was really tough – this was legally sanctioned access I was obliged to provide. There was no proof anything terrible was going on there – I figured he did things differently than I did, and he was justifiably angered by the fact I had rejected him. There was a lot of conflict between us and this made our children miserable. The kids were stuck in the middle and upset all the time. I had to deal with the über frustrating question: "What do I do with this?"

I tried everything that I could think of to try and get us onto more stable ground and, hey, I'm not perfect, I'm sure there were things I was doing that got his goat too. But although I like change, I did not like this state of affairs. The situation deteriorated and I engaged a psychologist to support my kids through the misery of warring parents. And things just kept getting worse.

I was stressed to the max and angry at the world. I felt that my kids were at risk and this was NOT OK! This was the hardest time of my life and I didn't know what to do.

I felt very alone and unsupported, abandoned even. I wasn't being heard and my kids weren't being heard, and, in desperation, I started to do a lot more energy work. That was the only thing I could think of to do and I tried with all my might just to be neutral. Eventually what got me through was the realization that my kids had chosen both of us to be their parents. All I could do was support them any way I could.

FREEDOM TIP #20:

I attracted my ex into my life for a reason: I have two beautiful, independent, kind, confident, loving and strong girls, and I also learned a lot about free will and choice. It all happened *for* me. You learn that your perception or opinion is your own. It is not up to you to convince anyone that you're correct or they are wrong. You can't make anyone do anything. We have free will. My resistance and frustration only attracted more of the same into my life. I began to accept the situation for the journey it was for me, just like everyone else gets to experience, only my unique version of it.

FREEDOM TIP #21:

YOU ARE NOT RESPONSIBLE OR HAVE ANY CONTROL OVER HOW SOMEONE ELSE IS FEELING! You can share from the most loving compassionate place and depending on what the information is, and what it triggers for another person, and what filters they run the information through, their reaction is dependent on how they feel. You are not responsible for anyone's feelings but your own.

I appreciate that the divorce and all that followed cannot have been easy for my ex and I don't want to minimize how difficult it is for men (or women) whose spouses have left them.

There is a huge amount of heartbreak either way, especially when there are children involved — unhappy children who might not agree with a state-ordered solution to their pain.

I reminded my children often that their dad loved them and explained that he was doing his best but having a hard time with this situation. I would often say to my kids, "your dad loves you as much as he can and he chooses not to learn new ways"

Finished Fighting

Two years ago, after a 10-year battle, we finished fighting about custody. My ego was wrapped up in a lot of what happened and it all happened *for* me, too. It was a very long, painful process.

My ex still reaches out to the girls once in a while – he wants to catch up – and there is still some healing to be done. He is doing his best to be the best father he can be and they are learning to forgive.

People get caught up in the drama and, tough as it is, you've got to sit there and not react. You've got to find neutrality with it all.

FREEDOM TIP #22:

If you want to flee… run towards yourself. Your pain is never about the other person.

Here's the truth: your children can't change who their parents are. That person is their biological birth parent, so if you say nasty things about your ex, or vice versa, you're making your kids feel bad about something they can do absolutely nothing to fix.

It's far more productive to help your kids see that their parent, step-parent, legal guardian, or whoever, is being the best person they can be at that time. If you're in a similar situation, I invite you to figure out what you can say to your kids that will support their relationship with the other parent without minimizing their need to be responsible for their own actions.

As I noted earlier, I'd often say to my girls, "your dad loves you as much as he can and he chooses not to learn new ways." I wonder what kind of things you could come up with ahead of time to say to your kids?

Here's the part about why change is good: if my kids hadn't had that experience with the divorce I doubt if they would be as open to living life in the flow, and living in joy and bliss and excitement, as they are now. The experience has helped them learn to become independent and determined. Resourceful and forgiving. Something better came out of that experience than they would have known had the relationship with their father been perceptively "perfect." It is also part of what catapulted me forward into remembering my own innate abilities and putting them into practice.

FREEDOM TIP #23:

If you have to speak your truth about something, check in with yourself, even write it down first to be sure you are coming from a place of love and compassion. When you speak from a place of needing to be right, you aren't coming from love. Do not engage in the Drama. If you're feeling reactive, sad, nervous, overwhelmed, or out of sorts, be kind and loving with yourself. These are big shifts!

It's like this: I remember when I was a little kid my parents and I were supposed to go on a vacation to Jamaica. We got to the airport and it turned out that there was a huge hurricane heading towards Jamaica.

My dad changed our plans at the last minute, and we ended up going to Hawaii. At that moment, everything switched. I even ended up eating French fries and drinking pop at an outdoor restaurant in Hawaii with Kristy McNichol, a superstar in those days. All by chance. The "Or Better" exists.

FREEDOM TIP #24:

Every morning before you get out of bed, just before your mind engages in what you have to get done for the day, say out loud or to yourself, "Something amazing is going to happen today. I wonder what it is?" And each night, before you go to sleep, get yourself a journal or a note pad and write down a minimum of five amazing things that happened during the day. (Some days it will be simple things like "I am breathing," or "the dog snuggled me,"; etc.)

FREEDOM TIP #25:

Your body doesn't know the difference between perceptive reality and imagination. Imagine yourself into what you want...and feel as though you are there. Voilà! You have shifted your vibration. You've changed the radio station. You are attracting in what you are vibrating out.

Chapter 9: Love, Fear & the Power of Prayer

I believe that every single event in life happens in an opportunity to choose love over fear.

- Oprah Winfrey

You can choose love or you can choose fear. And you don't ever have to defend yourself for the choice you make. At the same time, choosing love can give you a much richer experience, even though it might be perceptively uncomfortable.

It's almost as though we get tuned into one radio station and we stay on it for a long time. Remember that there are other stations out there, and they might be more enjoyable, or interesting or entertaining.

As long as we stick to that one familiar station, we will never know what else is possible for us.

You'd be surprised what happens when you give yourself permission to change the station: it allows life to start showing up differently for you.

The energy in the world has shifted a lot in the last few years and the shifts that have been happening can make life very uncomfortable and unfamiliar.

How Does Love Fit with Life?

When you're energetically committed to somebody else you have you, the other person, and a whole other entity you create together, a third living, breathing entity.

It's an energetic creation, and if one of you wants to disconnect from the arrangement, to move on somehow, there is an energy imbalance, and the other person can get very clingy or very unpleasant.

They feel the energetic unplugging and even though they don't know what's going on they can become very unhappy.

In my own experience of unplugging from my ex, it wasn't easy to hold him in a place of complete Divine love while I disconnected from him energetically. I had to get to a place of neutrality and to do that I had to do a lot of meditation, and a lot of travelling.

One exercise I did to support the process involved holding him in front of me energetically and having conversations of forgiveness with him.

I said to him, "For everything you've ever done to me in this life, or in any lifetime, in all directions, dimensions, and realities, that's perceptively brought me harm, I forgive you. And I humbly request forgiveness for anything I've ever done in any lifetime in all directions, dimensions, and realities, that's perceptively brought you harm, as well."

I blessed him, released him and sent him to the light.

What About Fear?

When we feel afraid it's only natural that we think about protecting ourselves. But maybe we don't need protection so much as we need to own the energy field of our lovingness. This is about being in a place of openness, and it involves our own willingness to listen to our higher levels, and to be brutally honest with ourselves about what our inner reality is showing us. When we release fearful energy that is no longer serving us, it creates the space for even more divine grace to come in. This is expansive and helps to dissolve fear that is buried deep down, locked away in places that you may have even forgotten. It relates to your ability to F.L.Y. (F.L.Y. = Fully Love Yourself).

Worrying is like Praying for What You Don't Want

When you focus on what you *do* want, and you're open to it being even better than you think it might be, and you avoid focusing on there being only one way for the plan to unroll, you will find that miracles happen all day long. They're all around us all the time, but if you're busy praying for what you don't want, then that's what you're going to get. It's really simple, although it's not always easy.

The truth is, we're always safe, although there's no proof. We just have to take that leap of faith into the knowledge that everything is going to be OK. You're totally safe and you're totally protected and your safety is coming from within you. We're just here for the experiences that give us the opportunity to release the stuff that's been internalized for a long time.

103

They help us to find ourselves in a place of total joy and appreciation. Life is not a test, and there are no "lessons" to learn. That belief comes from fear and failure and unworthiness, and the sense of not being enough. The Earth is one of the most beautiful places in the Universe; it's also one of the most dense places in the Universe, so it can be a perceptively uncomfortable place to be.

Facing Our Fears

I was part of an experiential awakening group a few years ago and we spent a lot of time dissolving many perceptively limiting issues, especially those related to fear. I started to see the times in my life when I had made choices and decisions from a place of ego. There were fears that I had had of being wrong, of not being heard, of being mis-understood. One part of the program took us to Cathedral Rock in Sedona Arizona.

This is a spectacular natural monument that you can climb up the rock to enjoy beautiful panoramic views of the countryside while experiencing vortex energy. I love climbing and I was determined to get to the top but there was one catch: when the group came to one part of the climb, a place I called the Ass Crack of the Rock, I froze in fear. This was a deep, very narrow fissure that divided the massive rock we were climbing into two pieces.

Down to the left was a very long drop to the Earth below and to the right the rock jetted up hundreds of feet straight up in the air. It was climbable. Apparently.

Two other members of our group were behind me and our group leader, Jennifer, who truly must have been a goat in another life, was already up the crack and no longer in sight.

I was pretty sure my husband, Bryan, was already up the crack as well. I politely told the others to go ahead and said that I was going to find a nice spot to meditate. That lasted about five minutes until I heard Jennifer calling my name. "Let's do this," she said sympathetically. She took me by the hand and before I knew what was happening I was back at the base of the Ass Crack. I was so scared I could no longer speak.

My hands were sweating, my legs were trembling and I was terrified. Jennifer told me to go back to when I was three years old....my mind started to scramble: I couldn't remember being three years old, I couldn't get it, and panic was starting to course through my body, Jennifer stood on the side where the cliff was and I pushed my body as close and tight up against the rock as I could. Then I heard her say "You're four, what would your four-year-old self do"?

Suddenly I was back and able to listen, and just at that moment a four-year-old boy jumped down from the Ass Crack and began telling his parents they were coming down too slow. I started to laugh a wee bit.

My hands were still quite sweaty but with Jennifer right behind me — and I mean right behind me, with her hand on my butt — I started to crawl and climb up the Ass Crack. The most amazing thing started to happen as people who were on their way down moved off to the side. They were all cheering me on. "You've got this...you're almost there... you're doing great!"

Complete strangers were cheering me on, reminding me that the Universe truly does have my back. I had tears streaming down my face, not from fear, but from the complete overwhelm of love that was being offered up to me, and that I humbly accepted.

I reached the top of the Ass Crack and let out the biggest cheer myself.

I was expecting to see all of the people who had gone up ahead of me, including my husband, and to my surprise, I was nowhere near the top. It was amazing how I then continued on this climbing journey, not feeling nearly as afraid as I had earlier. I had a new confidence that was somehow familiar.

I joined up with more group members and together we clambered up the difficult path to the top of the rock. Eventually, sweaty and out of breath, we could see the flat top of the rock just ahead.

As I took that last step and embraced the glorious feeling of making it to the top, this amazing breeze came up and caressed my face. It felt like the kiss of God. The view was beyond anything I'd ever seen. Every telomere in my body was singing and dancing as I connected and integrated with all the emotions and experiences of lifetimes of memories.

What If You Were Always Safe?

What if you could tap into that part of you that knows you are always safe and looked after? What if you could open up even more doors by dancing with what presents? What if you started to say YES instead of NO?

What if you opened up so much that the Universe could deliver everything you ever wanted and more? What if you began to receive so much that you could share it with the world to assist all of humanity?

What if all you need to be is you, *all* of who you are meant to be?

FREEDOM TIP #26:

Love is the Answer to Fear; when you hear the word "love" do you think of it as a soft squishy word? Does it make you feel warm inside? What if the word love was strong, courageous, contagious and firm? What if when fear came up around someone else's life choices, parenting, religion, politics, romance or sexuality, you could choose love? What if you could simply see those people as spiritual beings having an experience in a physical body and going about the journey they chose for themselves? What if you could let go of the fear filters through which you run things, and simply choose love?

 What if you could love them? You don't have to like people's behaviour but I invite you to go thousands of feet above the density of this 3D world and tap into the love we are all made of.

Seeing Scary Strangers as a Little Girl

One night, when I was three years old and my parents had company over, as they often did, I went up to my bedroom only to realize that my room was full of people. It was very noisy in my room and everyone seemed to want to talk at the same time. I could see only parts of some people and there was something unfamiliar about all of them.

I called my mom into my bedroom and asked why all the people were in my room. She was a little perplexed: she didn't see anybody and she said that all the people were in the living room. She asked me to describe the people. Well, I did my best but I was three, with not too much context for describing what I was seeing.

107

I said that the people looked kind of like Popeye and a few other cartoon characters. My mom discussed the situation with my dad down the hall and they decided that I was no longer allowed to watch cartoons.

Then they labeled me "over sensitive." There was an aura of disapproval around what I had shared with my parents and it all taught me to keep mum about what I was seeing. It started an energy within me that I would later label as "fear."

And Then There Is Love

When we make decisions out of fear we are almost guaranteed to bring the roof down on our heads because fear is not an expansive emotion and it confines us to a set of circumstances that keep us small. If I had not overcome my terror of climbing up the Ass Crack I would never have gone on to experience the glorious feeling of making it to the very top of Cathedral Rock. I'd have missed the sense of inspired connection to the planet and the love I felt for all humanity. Love is where it's at, Baby, and it feels so much different than fear!

FREEDOM TIP #27:

Take a few nice deep breaths and see that through it all, there is this calm and love that pervades if you simply listen and feel inside.

I can remember the day I found out I was pregnant with my beautiful first-born, Kylee. I was scheduled for surgery the next morning to have a cyst removed from my ovaries; it was the size of a cantaloupe.

I had had surgery in the past to remove tissue that had gotten outside of my uterus and was growing on my fallopian tubes. After that last operation, the specialist had told me that I would never be able to have children. I was devastated by this news. I had spent seven years working with street-entrenched youth in an emergency care home in Vancouver's downtown core. These kids had all been dealt some interesting cards and it was an honour to be a part of their lives. I absolutely loved children of all ages and I always thought that I would have some of my own some day.

The night before the surgery I was feeling funny, like something was about to happen. I remember telling my boyfriend that something just wasn't sitting right. I took four pregnancy tests that night and, predictably, they were all negative. I could feel a presence around me and I couldn't get a clear picture of what that really was. I gave it all up to the Universe and went to bed. My boyfriend took me to the hospital and got me checked in. Hospital staff took urine and blood samples for the surgery and then set me up in a room. I sent my boyfriend off with the understanding that he didn't have to be back until I was out of surgery, expected to be sometime around 3:30pm.

A nurse started wheeling my bed down the hall towards the operating room. My IV was in and I was all set to go. Another nurse behind us started calling to us to come back. I was very upset — the surgery had already been postponed once and I didn't want them to change the plan again. The nurse spun the bed around to face the other way and the other nurse came up and said, "The doctor wants to talk to you." I was super agitated by this and kept going on and on about the surgery and how I really didn't want to wait. Finally, the nurse blurted out "You're pregnant!" I said, "I can't be pregnant; you must have gotten my urine mixed up with someone else's." Just then the doctor came in and with a lovely Irish accent and said, "Now isn't that a wee bit of good news?"

I was in shock. I was just lying in this bed looking at the doctor, like *"Whaaaaaat?"* He explained I wouldn't be getting the surgery and that I would be just fine.

It Was a Miracle

The doctor said he'd seen this type of thing before and there was no scientific explanation. It was a miracle. He'd just left when my mother came around the corner to wish me luck with my surgery. I told her that I wasn't going for surgery. "Why not?" she asked.

"I'm pregnant," I said. My mom started to cry and then my sister came into the room and she started to cry. I was still in shock and so freaking hungry! My mom and I got out of the hospital and went for a big breakfast. It was starting to sink in... I was pregnant!

It was the best day of my life. Nothing else mattered; I was so excited to be pregnant. My boyfriend had a hard time dealing with the pregnancy but he did eventually propose and we did get married. Throughout that pregnancy I would look down at my belly and sigh, then smile and marvel to myself, "I am having a baby!" I was grateful and full of love for the little being striving to start claiming her life from her little home inside me.

I spent the last six weeks of that pregnancy in hospital with toxemia and I had a C-section induced, but my life became an ode to love the moment Kylee was born.

One year later I was pregnant again. I had a lot of fear the second time around: I was afraid that the pregnancy would be the same as my first one and I was also afraid that I wouldn't have as much love for another child. I mean, how could I?

My heart was bursting with love for the baby I already had. I put my fears aside and experienced the easiest pregnancy ever. The last few months of the pregnancy I had to go for ultrasounds each week because I couldn't feel the baby moving.

And, having had a C-section the first time, I had no idea what going into labour felt like or what to expect.

When I finally went in to labour, I remember waiting for the pain to get so bad that I couldn't handle it anymore. I mean, all the horror stories I had been told were rattling around in my head scaring the jeepers out of me.

The next thing I knew the nurse was telling me that I was fully dilated and I could start pushing. I gave birth to a beautiful baby girl who we named Cassidy. I was wrong to wonder if I would be capable of loving another child as much as the first.

My heart overflowed with love for all of my children – the ones to whom I gave birth and the ones who became part of my family when I married Bryan.

Choosing Love

It was three weeks before our August wedding and Bryan and I were on a pre-honeymoon holiday with four of our five kids at Disney World in Florida. We'd been together for years, but we had maintained separate households because Bryan's kids had not been on board with us being together in a permanent kind of way.

Bryan's ex-wife was struggling with our relationship and his kids were behaving terribly. Our wedding was scheduled to take place on a day Bryan would have his kids two weeks after we returned to Canada but his three children were still not coping well with our relationship. None of them planned to be at the wedding.

Emotions were high and intense. Bryan and I managed to grab a few minutes alone together one evening down by the pool and I told him that I loved him immensely, more than I ever thought possible. Although our wedding was imminent, I let him know that I didn't want him to marry me and then become resentful and unhappy because his kids were not on board with our relationship or our marriage.

The cost of keeping two residences going was ridiculous, but we wanted to give his kids the opportunity to come to terms with our relationship in their own time. Like many divorced dads, he was afraid that he might lose his kids and the bonds that held them together. I told him that if he wanted to back out of our engagement, I would totally understand. We talked for about an hour and went over how difficult things were for him and for his kids.

The following evening Bryan came to me and said "I love you to the moon and back" (which I had never doubted). "If I chose not to marry you, I would become resentful of my children. They're almost grown. Should I give up the woman I love so I can grow old alone and bitter because of the choices I made? No! I want to marry you, and no matter what I do I have no control over what my kids think or do; they may never accept our relationship. I can't control that. All I can do is love them unconditionally. Do I choose love or fear? "I choose love for all."

FREEDOM TIP #28:

Some people may come into your life but not always be front and centre. Just know they're connected to you and as you step forward into who you are with love and grace, they'll feel the effects of that love. They may seem to fall away from your inner circle, but are on the outer edge of the circle, watching from a distance to be sure it's safe for them to dance in this divine grace.

FREEDOM TIP #29:

It's not so much about what you love; it's seeing the love in everything. I know this sounds hippyish, but when you can see that it all comes from love and loving everyone and everything without expectation or an attachment to an outcome, everything expands.

We had the most beautiful wedding imaginable and although Bryan's kids decided not to come, we celebrated our love and commitment to each other our own way.

This man had seen every side of me and I married him for the love that he is.

He totally "got me" without wanting to change anything about me. I am so in love with him.

After we said our vows, and I stopped crying, we all looked up and saw a beautiful eagle flying above us. Then there were two, then three, and finally we had five eagles circling above us, so close. Bryan and I looked at each other and in that moment, we knew we were supported in our union.

The entire Universe had conspired to bring us together and, in a way, we felt those five eagles represented our five children and the circle of love we had created with our family.

FREEDOM TIP #30:

Sometimes it feels like there's a hurricane, and you are caught up in the wind. You've got to get yourself back into the eye of the hurricane, quiet your mind, and decide whether you are going to come from love or fear. You can choose whether to come from love or fear – it's simple, although it's not always easy.

FREEDOM TIP #31:

To F.L.Y. (Fully love yourself), requires compassion for where you are on your journey and FYI there is no destination. When you fully love yourself, you FLY ~ everything else just melts away.

Chapter 10: Limiting Beliefs and Limitations

Be the kind of woman that when your feet hit the floor each morning, the devil says, "oh crap, she's up!

- Author Unknown

The greatest fear in the world is of the opinions of others, and the moment you are unafraid of the crowd, you are no longer a sheep. You become a lion. A great roar arises in your heart, the roar of freedom.

- Osho

Your eyes can't see the light directly, only the things it shines upon, so the light remains invisible, just like the soul does.

- Annie Kagan

My older sister and I were enjoying playing with our Barbie house one day when a disagreement erupted and we started arguing. We were little girls. I was younger than age 10, my sister four years older. This was just one in a long line of angry outbursts for us and, in a fit of frustration, my sister yelled at me the words that would become imprinted on my brain for decades to come: "I wish you were never born! I wish my brother was still alive! He would be here instead of you!"

I was stunned into silence and I was totally confused. I had no idea what she was talking about. I found my mom and told her what my sister had said. I found out that my mom had given birth to another baby in between my older sister and me. She had carried him to full term, birthed him, named him and buried him. His name was Joseph.

The effect the entire story had on me was very powerful. I was here instead of Joseph, but he had been the wanted sibling, not me. That feeling of being "unwanted" grew, and as time went on I collected more evidence to prove that I was a second-class citizen in my family and in my world. I created a lot more beliefs that limited my outlook on my place in life:

1. You're unlovable.

2. You're not enough.

3. You're not what we wanted – we wanted a boy.

4. You don't fit in.

5. Keep it to yourself, no one will believe you and they will take things away.

6. You're over-sensitive.

7. You're weird and you see things others don't see. That's not normal.

All too often, we don't question what we believe or why we do things a certain way. I'm sure you've heard the story of unquestioning acceptance that happened in someone's kitchen one day.

A six-year-old girl was helping her mom prepare a roast for dinner and the little girl watched as her mom cut the tip of the roast off.

"Why do you always cut that part off?" she asked her mom. Her mom sat and thought about it for a while and then said, "Well, that's how grandma always did it, so why don't we ask her at dinner tonight?"

When grandma arrived the little girl asked her "Why do you and mommy always cut the tip of the roast off?" Grandma replied, "I don't know why your mom does it but I used to cut it off because my roasting pan was too small to fit the roast."

Beliefs Are Like Habits

When I was growing up, some of my dad's favorite sayings included "money doesn't grow on trees," which is a fact, and "you have to work hard for your money," which is more of a belief – not a fact. But when we hear them often enough we absorb them into our neurology and operate from their wisdom as though they were true.

It is so easy to adopt other people's stuff!

As beautiful beings of light, when we come into this world we have already taken on generations of beliefs.

Before you were born, your parents had all kinds of well-intended expectations for you. Or, maybe they had to give you up for adoption, which set up some beliefs in your psyche. Or, perhaps their parents came from an abusive background... whatever line you were born from, there are undoubtedly a packet of limiting, fear-based beliefs that attached themselves to your energy.

117

These limiting beliefs and expectations were never yours to begin with, and some of them go really far back, lifetimes even. They can affect what you attract into your life.

Let's take some examples: "money doesn't grow on trees" and "you have to work hard for your money." If you believe those statements to be true, then you will never blast through them and discover that money can come quickly and easily. So I changed those statements to "Money comes to me quickly and easily, and all of my needs are cared for."

Remember that our beliefs give rise to our thoughts — whether they are empowering or fearful—and they are powerful. They are the key to the kind of life we are busy co-creating with the Universe at every moment of every day. Our thoughts can generate a life full of grace and ease or it can create a life full of challenge and misery. Choose your thoughts and you choose your life.

For example, what if Hell were actually a concept that humanity has created simply by thinking it into existence through our fears and limiting beliefs?

What if Heaven were actually a concept we've thought into existence through our hopes and empowering beliefs? The answer to the question of "What is Reality?" is beyond the scope of this book. And many highly-educated people have spent lifetimes examining the issue.

For now, I'd like to leave you with the understanding that you can influence your enjoyment of life simply by focusing your thoughts and beliefs on the kind of life you actually want to live.

FREEDOM TIP #32:

The Universe doesn't know the difference between imagination and reality. This is a huge key to freedom. Whatever you are vibrating and emanating out because of what you are imagining or observing, the Universe will respond and bring back the perfect match to that vibration so your vibration is what attracts what you have showing up in your life. Your emotion is your guide to what you are vibrating out. You see "what you focus on expands." check your emotion with things and you will know what is coming. Imagine something believable.

Invite New Opportunities

These old limiting beliefs that people hang onto can take up residence within them as entities that disrupt their energy. You might be doing everything you can think of to do to keep yourself clear – repeating positive thoughts and affirmations, and so on, and this might go on for days and weeks. But nothing changes. "Why isn't it shifting?" you wonder. Well, sometimes your limiting beliefs are so entangled within you that you would benefit from some assistance in disentangling and releasing them.

These beliefs are the aspects of an individual that can move and shift and leave so they are no longer affecting your physical reality. These beliefs, these entities, can, over time, cover up and extinguish who a person truly is and make them forget who they are on the planet to be.

119

And so the key is to trust that you're being looked after. Interference? Yeah, that's real, and it's just a question of peeling away those layers to free yourself from negative influences. You can do it in this lifetime but if you choose not to do it that's perfect, too – you'll be back sometime for more.

It's interesting – everyone wants to know what their purpose is. All of humanity's purpose is simply to release the density, release the limiting beliefs and remember who we are, remember our own bright light and shine that light without judgement and without fear. It is so simple.

However, the mind and the logic, which have no place in our spiritual understanding, get in the way. And they can make it feel not-so-easy. This is the piece that the ego contributes: the logic, the mind, and the fear. Our egos were created from fear, and we call them into reality as beings in and of themselves. They don't have to be so large and in charge. Your ego can be small. It does serve some purpose. But it's a very minimal purpose at this time. It is of more service to those who are just starting on their journey of remembering. Remembering to fly. As I've said before, Fully Love Yourself. FLY!

FREEDOM TIP #33:

Give your ego a name, something weak — maybe name it after a cartoon or character from a book or T.V. show. My ego's name used to be Barney after the big purple dinosaur. Then my kids gave it the name of Bevy from a T.V. show. Thank your ego (by name) for reminding you of the fear… and do it anyway!

The Power of Meditation

I highly recommend meditations to get people started on releasing their limiting beliefs. I offer meditations in my Freedom Shop that can assist in releasing you from many limiting beliefs through relaxing and following along, or simply playing them while you're sleeping. My meditations are really more like clearings. Early on in my journey of awakening I tried many types of meditation and could never get what it was all about. What I have learned is that you can't get it wrong.

The technique I use doesn't require a lot of know-how. When people first start it sometimes takes a few tries before they start relaxing into the concept. The important part isn't what I am saying in the meditations, as much as what is happening on a quantum level. Things that have been holding you back will be released regardless of whether you are aware of them or not. You may get the impulse to drift off on your own without following the guidance in the meditation and that is perfect as well. It's all about getting yourself familiar with the feeling of tapping into the other dimensions. Astro travelling is a way of tapping into the many different dimensions that are all around us. It can help you release anxiety, panic, illness and much more.

It does happen sometimes that some fear-based beliefs and memories may creep in to your life. For example, someone who has never been afraid of water, swims up until they're 30 years old, and all of a sudden they develop a tremendous fear of swimming. This is what is called cell memory and it usually relates to other lifetimes they have lived. Help is available for getting over something like that.

121

It's important to remember as well that what we believe things should look like sometimes limits us. One of my clients has been creating a story of what they believe a love relationship should look like for many years. Hers is more of a fairy tale story than anything else and the facts of her life aren't supporting either her imagination or her desire to make her dream a reality. It's not to say that your desire cannot be fulfilled, however it may not be with the beloved you would prefer. And the relationship might not look the way you believe it should look. The key is to be open to things the way they are without expectation or judgement, and loving where you are, even if it doesn't match the fantasy.

FREEDOM TIP #34:

If you are not attracting what you want then you are simply not vibrating out the frequency of what you want. It may not be an energetic match at this time. As your frequency shifts and changes, so does what shows up in your life.

Sometimes, when you get so stuck in what you think something should be like, you miss the part about how it has nothing to do with the other person. Your life is solely about you and how you're looking at things, and how you're perceiving them, as opposed to how they are showing up for you. So, this is a time to ask some questions. Sometimes these things are catalysts that we've buried. For example, why have you attracted someone into your life who is unattainable and unavailable? What are your beliefs around yourself and around a love relationship?

Anyway, back to my client. She was struggling with what she believed a romantic relationship should look like. She was thinking fairy tale thoughts and beginning to recognize that it was like she was on the inside of a wheel and running the same story but expecting a different result. She was running and running but until she was willing to see beyond the little radar that she'd created, she was destined to keep running in that circle. There were many mid-point things happening behind the scenes that helped her to see a different story. And eventually she did break through to realize what she wanted was a true story, not a fantasy. But she had a lot of beliefs to release first and that work positioned her for a joyfulness she could never have imagined when she was struggling to make the fairy tale come true.

FREEDOM TIP #35:

I wonder how many things you have taken on that were never really yours to begin with? Looking back through your life, what are some of the beliefs you have taken on to be yours? What if you took that list and asked who all those beliefs belonged to? What if most of what we believe isn't our own belief? What if you could send those beliefs back to the beginning of Consciousness? What if somewhere along the way you convinced yourself they are all your beliefs? What if you could ask your higher levels (The Universe, God, angels, guides etc.) to send it back? Try it and see how much lighter you may feel. Next, find a piece of paper, or better yet, a journal, and write down the beliefs you're aware of, then take that list of limiting beliefs and turn them around. Create and write out your own mantras – feel them, experience what you want.

FREEDOM TIP #36:

Left hand on heart; deep belly breath in pulling in all those beautiful packets of light. Breathing in love and breathing out love as you release those feelings with love. Thank you. You are safe. There are no lessons; there is no one who wants to bring you down to find your faults. It is simply important to just remember who you truly are.

FREEDOM TIP #37:

When given a choice about anything, look at it without the ego and decide to choose either Love or Fear. That's not to say that if you choose love you won't feel fear. Most likely you will feel fear; push through without expectations of how it should look. Control and expectations are what keep us stuck. They are ultimately from the ego and indicate a lack of trust in the fact that the Universe truly has your back.

Chapter Eleven: Judgement and Forgiveness

When you release the judgement, what is there to forgive?

- Kaayla Vedder

The things we focus on and judge about others are the very things in us we are afraid to look at in ourselves. It is never about the other person.

- Kaayla Vedder

Have you ever met someone and judged them before you have even given them a chance to show you who they truly are? Right off the bat, you are feeling that you don't like them.

Maybe they have triggered a perceptively negative memory of someone who had the same hair color, or maybe the same vehicle, as someone who you felt had been perceptively untrustworthy.

Maybe they smile "too much" or their mouth seems to be frozen in a permanent sneer. For whatever reason, you just don't trust them. You spend time running everything about this person through the filters you've created to make yourself right about your opinion, and voilà, you are correct. You will always find evidence to prove you are correct.

Somewhere along the line we humans have decided that there is a right way and a wrong way to do things. It could be around anything.

We've created all kinds of judgments based on old limiting beliefs that we developed through experiences from our past, whether they occurred in this lifetime or a previous one. We've learned that things have to be a certain way, and if they aren't, and/or you don't fit into the mold that humanity has cast for you, then something must be wrong with you.

Newsflash: you're not broken and you don't need to be fixed. These judgments are the very things that keep us hooked into the drama of our stories.

You see, we tend to create expectations based on our family's and our society's beliefs. We take them on and create judgments about what we think people should be like. But these are ancient beliefs and the judgements are very damaging.

So, although your behaviour triggers a judgemental reaction in someone else, "you" are not "bad." In fact, chances are good that you are triggering experiences for yourself that will broaden your heart and deepen your soul. These are just experiences. And everything is happening *for* us, not *to* us. When we let go of our expectations, there are no judgments.

And PS, what is there to forgive if there is no judgment?

And by the way, what if you are that jerk who agreed to be here to be a jerk? Or the Negative Nelly who is here to irritate other people into becoming more positive people? It takes greater courage to be a perceptively unpleasant person on the planet than it does to be an angel. It's easy to be the person everybody likes. That's no big deal. But to be the person that triggers everybody else? That takes guts.

And we have to remember, as well, that when you judge others, it's never about them. It's always about you. I can't say this enough.

Here's the thing: what if we are given the opportunity to experience *all* of the emotions that are available to us? And what if we could have all kinds of emotions rise and fall without examining them or needing to be right? We could simply experience them. When we experience emotion, a lot of times we will decide to examine them and then even, at times, blame others for how we are feeling.

But you are not the emotion, you are this beautiful extension of Source, the Universe, God, whatever you want to call it. From what I see, we all have this beautiful bundle of light that comes shooting in with our soul when we are taking human form. This same beautiful light exits our body when we are complete with this physical form. We never really die.

FREEDOM TIP #38:

It's never about the other person, place or thing. It's all you baby!

Every particle of divine light expands into and out to all. It affects the whole. Who we came here to be is affecting others as well. The "you" you are here to emanate is the "you" that plays and expands, affecting the whole.

When you're being who you truly are, and you're clearing the energy for you, you're clearing it for all of humanity. It is fractally impossible not to.

Bullies in the Schoolyard

When I was in public school, my mother ended up with a job as the principal's secretary in the office and because of that a lot of the other kids thought I was getting special treatment. Little did they know how NOT special the treatment I got at home and school was! And so they started bullying me. Even the teachers didn't seem to know what to do. The staff had all decided to make sure that I didn't get any special treatment, and in fact they were harder on me just to prove how "fairly" I was being treated.

I remember thinking "What the heck is going on here?! Why is everyone so mean and unhappy?"

It dawned on me much later that these kids had spent a great amount of time learning how to be what and who they were expected to be, and if anyone was different from what they had been taught was acceptable, that person must be wrong, bad, and incorrect.

Now, I wasn't angry with everything that was going on. I was truly saddened. But it gave me a much greater appreciation for just how easy it is for people to misunderstand one another.

You Can't Get It Wrong

There are a million ways to be on this journey of awakening and none of them are wrong

If someone has an opinion of me and they say, "You're weird," or "You're wrong," or "You're a strang cookie," or whatever it is – then I say to them: "Yeah, and it's OK."

As far as they're concerned, they're right in their opinion and unless I take it on to affect my opinion, it doesn't touch me.

They don't have to convince me they're right and I don't have to make them wrong in order for me to be right.

Marriages split up because one person needs to be right. But both parties could be right.

When you're fighting to be right it's like you know all the answers – and when you figure you know all the answers, then you're cutting yourself off from Source.

Arguments always have a trigger but it's never about the trigger. Something happens and you get stuck in the drama, maybe telling your story over and over to other people.

You're actually looking to be validated, to be told that you're in the right, and that the other person is wrong. Validation lets you play the victim.

When you can totally, nakedly, look at yourself and what's really going on, and let the story go, you can release the issue and allow yourself to receive beautiful divine grace. Because it's not about the story.

FREEDOM TIP #39:

If you're experiencing what seems to be a blockage in a relationship, hold that person in your mind's eye; let go of the need for anyone to be right/wrong; good or bad; drop all the judgement of yourself and simply feel the emotions. They are a "trigger" for you; catapulting you forward in your own awakening; they are there to assist you in remembering your own knowing.

The Hawaiian Dog

When I went to Hawaii with my parents as a child (and met actress Kristy McNichol, as I mentioned earlier!) I had many awarenesses and activations that made a big impression on me. What a trip! This place was beautiful. My dad rented a car and made a plan to tour the beaches.

We stopped at one beach and saw that there were no others cars in the parking lot. The beach seemed to be deserted, and there were signs saying "Undertow — swim at your own risk." We were planning to enjoy a picnic lunch and, being the explorer that I am, I wandered off down the beach with my lunch in hand.

I found a nice spot just at the edge of the beach and I was taking a moment to soak in the sun and enjoy the sounds of the surf when I heard a little whimpering sound. Just down the beach was a little wiener-type dog. I kept calling him to come closer and even offered him a piece of my sandwich. He eventually snuggled up next to me and I proceeded to feed him my lunch. He was covered in fleas and dirt and didn't look too good.

I took him back to my parents and declared that he was coming with us! A big argument ensued, and I simply stood my ground and stated that we couldn't leave him there all alone.

My dad (who truly is a gentle soul) agreed, but complained about how grotty the dog looked and how awful it was going to be for us to take him back to the hotel. And so on. Well, the Universe must have had his back that day, because just as we were about to leave, a police officer pulled up and asked how we were doing? My dad said "Great, except that my daughter found this dog on the beach..."

130

The officer pointed out that wasn't a very popular beach so someone must have dumped the dog there. "It's not uncommon," he said. He was just finishing up his shift and he agreed to take the dog and put it on his enclosed porch for the night; then he would take it to a shelter in the morning.

It truly dawned on me at that moment that I was like the dog: I really didn't fit in. I remember looking around at my family that day and thinking "who are these people?"

Don't get me wrong I truly love my family, and, actually, I have always felt a profound love for all of humanity. But, like that little lost dog, somehow I just didn't fit.

FREEDOM TIP #40:

You made a plan with all of these people who are in your life before you came into your physical body. You and they agreed to play these roles from such a place of euphoric love, all with the intention of assisting you to remember all of who you are. Then you came into your physical body and experienced amnesia. Wake up! You are not your story or experiences, you're so much more!

Years Later Things Still Didn't Fit

My parents eventually split up and my dad drifted away from us kids. As an adult, not too long ago, after five years of not seeing my dad, I met up with him and his second wife. This is a lady who used to be my mom's best friend and I can tell you there were certainly opportunities for me to be judgemental in that situation.

I realize from 30,000 feet above the density that you can't fit a square peg in to a round hole. It was enlightening to be sitting beside my father and seeing his own struggles. I love him and his light and I am so blessed that he and his wife, my sister, my mother and everyone else in my family, chose to be on my journey with me.

They've all done and said things to further my process. Even today, I don't fit in with my biological family and I am totally OK with that.

And what about you? Do you fit in?

Or are there people in your life who you have judged based on past experiences with others?

Have you ever judged yourself and come up short?

What if you could release these memories and experiences so that you could allow even more grace and divine love to enter your light?

FREEDOM TIP #41:

Pick one day of the week and say, "I'm not going to judge myself or anyone else today." If you catch yourself judging yourself, stop it! Just say, "Thank you for showing me what I have left to release" and be grateful for it, whatever it is. You see, when you judge others, the judgement is never about the other person. It's always about you. Nothing is ever about the other person. I can't say this enough. Evolution is about having courage and a willingness to surrender your judgements so you can see these are simply ways in which you are still holding yourself back.

FREEDOM TIP #42:

You can do this with one person or a bunch of people. In your mind's eye see the person(s) in front of you. If it is too painful, and you don't want to picture them, then simply see their light, without their physical body. Say out loud, or in your head, "I forgive you for all of the things you have perceptively ever done to me in any life in all directions in all dimensions. I humbly request your forgiveness for anything I have ever done to you in any life time in all directions in all dimensions. And so it is." Then watch the person, or their light, go to the brighter light. Bless and release. It really is simple, however it is not always easy.

FREEDOM TIP #43:

When you have dropped all judgement, there is no longer any energy left to hold them as a "trigger," it simply melts away. Ahh sigh… the FREEDOM you have created.

FREEDOM TIP #44:

When you're busy blaming someone else for something, it's really the Universe giving you the opportunity to say, "thank you for showing me what I still hold to be true for me." You can dive in and dissect it or you can simply Bless and Release.

Chapter Twelve: Ego Versus Flow

Comparison is the thief of Joy.

- Theodore Roosevelt

When something presents itself to you, and you simply surrender to it, everything is easy.

You feel no resistance and, even if you do resist, you find that if you take any small bit of action, the situation unfolds a little more, and takes on a life of its own. That's what being in flow is like.

As long as you are coming from a place of love, expansion and surrender, no matter what you do, you cannot get it wrong.

My wonderful dog, Wrigley, became seriously ill about a year ago and I couldn't bear the thought of being without him. The vet said it looked like a brain tumour and I resisted doing the tests that would have confirmed it. Wrigley is a special guy and he's been with me and my family through some very interesting and challenging years.

I cried a lot when we first found out that there might be something life-threatening happening with Wrigley, in fact I cried solidly for three days. And I questioned everything. How much pain can one person bear, right? I'm sure you've been there, too. The tears and the pain were all triggers for me to ask a lot of questions, and find some answers.

All of this allowed me to release a lot of emotional stuff that was buried so deep that I was no longer crying for Wrigley alone, I was crying for humanity.

Eventually, I started to notice that I had let go of any expectations of what Wrigley's journey was going to look like, and I started to trust that whatever was necessary was going to happen.

It wasn't easy for me to let go and let God take care of it all. I think that if I had decided that Wrigley was going to die of a brain tumor then he probably would have died of a brain tumor.

However, what happened was that I let go of what it was going to look like and everything shifted. Things can shift in a moment, a millisecond, and I became OK with what was happening. Wrigley is still with us today, still content to curl up on his bed beside my desk in the office, still prancing excitedly up the hiking trails behind our home in beautiful British Columbia when we go for a walk. I know there will come a time when he transitions on to whatever comes next for dogs and hearts. But the experience taught me a lot.

People are always looking for the answers outside of themselves and those messages definitely *are* given to us. You are human. Question everything. As humans, we want answers... the answers we seek don't come with physical evidence, we require a belief in something you can't see... that's about faith — otherwise it would be called proof.

Whether they're legitimate or not, the messages that come to you can change your thoughts and beliefs — which can change the outcome of a situation — in a heartbeat. It's about staying in flow.

FREEDOM TIP #45:

Know that you will get the guidance you require. You're going to get it by listening to the whispers of the Universe or the louder nudges it sends next, or by the cosmic two-by-four that demands your attention.

And the Ego Says...

Ahh, sigh... the ego... that beautiful ego and its constant effort to keep us perceptively safe. What if you are *always* safe? What if your ego is so afraid of you learning that surrendering delivers nothing that should be feared, that it goes into high gear whenever you decide to move forward in your journey of awakening?

The ego loves to keep things separate and dualistic. It revels in judgements of right and wrong, judgements of ourselves and others, and the separateness of "better-than less-than." These are distinctions the ego feels it has to make in order to make us feel OK with ourselves.

What if we are already OK? What if we are already so amazing that we don't require any artificial support for our self-worth? Much of our language is dualistic: we have the words fearful/courageous, weak/strong, right/wrong, male/female, good/bad... you get the idea... and they keep us separate and, if we're on the "right" side of the continuum, they also keep us perceptively safe. It seems as if these words are of the ego, they are of fear. These words don't occur or even enter our being-ness when we are simply awake. Nothing is wrong with us when we are feeling any of those emotions, however judging creates stress anxiety. When judgement is absent, and we are experiencing everything in the absence of duality, we are awake!

Saying Yes

I had a recent conversation with a client, who was feeling upset and not sure about attending a program I was hosting. I told her that she was an amazing being of light. "Your little ego is having a hissy fit," I said. "This is very common when someone is on the verge of a breakthrough, and it can be very uncomfortable."

I've worked with numerous people who were feeling the same as this lady and I've realized that when you're venturing out to make connections with your soul family (people who get you and love you for who you are and where you are on your journey *without judgement*), then the ego will come up with all kinds of excuses to hold you back in familiar territory. But when these people came to the event, their ego settled down.

So, I advised this lady to thank her ego, push it aside and ask her higher levels if the program was in the highest for her to attend. When you get a "Yes!" internally to something like that, thank your ego and let it know you're doing it anyway.

The important thing to remember is that when you say yes, the journey begins. A lot of old beliefs come up to go. You are much farther along the path of awakening than you know, and you have a lot to offer. We are all assisting each other, whether we are aware of it or not.

The great thing about the Universe and how it works is that you can never get it wrong. You will always be redirected to whatever is in the highest for you. You can go with the flow or go kicking and screaming. Whatever you decide, you'll go forward in your journey. We're all assisting each other to awaken to our own amazingness. You have your own unique piece to offer humanity.

Have you ever felt exhausted by the craziness going on around you? Have you ever experienced emotional outbursts, a confused mind and even an aching body?

Everything of the density must go for everyone in order for the planet to wake up. Fear projections of all kinds are reflected and deflected immediately back to us. It all has to come up because none of us can bring any baggage with us.

So, allow it all. Deal with the emotion, let it out in private or with someone with whom you can share, someone who can listen with loving ears and who doesn't try to solve anything for you. Remember that as the old reality leaves of its own accord, it allows room for the New to flow in. Do not take any of it seriously, and remember that it is real until it is Not: you are the Creator of your own reality.

All that we are experiencing is called "being human," in other words, living fully as a Human Being. It is all God, it is all part of the rich fabric of you and me. So we are at last allowing and befriending it all.

FREEDOM TIP #46:

Fear is what keeps you where you are. Pushing past the fear and doing things anyway will assist you to propel yourself forward into more of who you are. It's not that successful people don't feel fear; it's that they feel fear and do it anyway.

FREEDOM TIP #47:

What is being mirrored back to you? This is what you are vibrating out.

Which Brings Us Into Flow

Whether you realize it or not, you're putting your order in to the Universe every minute of every day. The Universe will respond, but every time you change your order there is so much that has to go on before the order can be filled.

We want things when we want them and we usually want them NOW! You put your order in, get frustrated with waiting, change your order – and the Universe has to start all over again.

But if you're in a place of flow, you put your order in, surrender the process to the Universe, take a little action, and the Universe responds.

When Bryan and I realized we were a committed couple and we wanted to live comfortably together, we wrote a list of everything we wanted in a new home: we wanted a private bit of property that we could easily afford.

We didn't want to have to do any more construction, it had to be a turn-key deal. We put our order in and kept looking, until one day, about a year after our search began, I was sitting at the computer and I found our new home. It took a while to convince Bryan to go look at it but when we saw this place we were smitten.

The interior had been totally redone and although there was some yard work to do, we put in our offer and after a little bit of negotiating, which involved the trailer we were then living in, the house was ours.

If something you want in your life is not coming through for you, then it means that you are not a vibrational match for whatever it is that you want to attract in to your life.

Ask yourself, "What part of me doesn't believe I deserve this?" What if you don't believe it's possible? If you're a total sceptic and you're digging your heels in, then it's time to consider surrendering. Your beliefs are what limit you – it's important to be a vibrational match for what you're putting out there.

I start my days asking: "How could my life possibly get better than this? What else is possible? Something amazing will happen today – I wonder what it is?"

Your perfect life doesn't have to look like what everyone else thinks it should look like. Just focus on being in flow. It's all God. Just say "yes." Whatever it is, say "yes." What if a dream-come-true for you is knocking on your door and you keep saying no?

If the Universe has your back, what on Earth do you have to worry about? You have to let go of the worry and the control. When you think you're in control and you are busy creating a future that doesn't exist, this is when anxiety can hit.

Breathe and take a moment to pay attention to your breath, give your mind a job and get back into this moment.

And What About Expectations?

Expectations are almost always disappointing. Have you ever had the experience of a friend encouraging you to go see a movie she has just seen? She tells you that it was the best movie *ever*.

However, when you watch the movie you feel let down because you were expecting an amazing movie and what you got was just *meh* okay.

Your friend went in to the movie with no expectations. You, on the other hand… are disappointed.

The fewer expectations we have in life, the less disappointment we experience. Step into the unfamiliar! If you have no expectations, you have no idea what's coming around the corner. You will get to be surprised.

Fear of a situation is just the ego talking. There's nothing to fear. If something is unfamiliar, that doesn't mean it's wrong. We're not supposed to live our lives doing the same thing over and over and expecting something different to happen. That's the definition of insanity.

If you expect to get different results, you have to take different action. When an opportunity presents to step into the unfamiliar, allow yourself to feel the fear and say, "thank you." The most profound shifts happen on the other side of "comfortable."

Flow and Marriage

It was a big decision to leave my previous husband and if you've ever been in that situation you'll know how challenging it is to take that final step.

Sure, there were plenty of reasons to leave him, not least of which was the fact that I wasn't in love with him. But I had truly wanted this relationship to work for the sake of my kids.

When I chose to leave him, I wrote a note to the Universe and I was very specific: "If it's in the highest for me to leave," I said in my note, "then I want a full-time job that I enjoy doing, and I want a house I can easily afford with a yard for a dog that is housebroken and easily cared for."

142

Within a couple of days, I was picking my kids up from school when one of the moms asked me what was new. "I'm going to start looking for a job," I said. The other mom immediately got excited and said "The company I work for is looking for someone to take over the corporate sales position. Are you interested? *Was* I?! Oh YEAH!!!

Within weeks I interviewed with the company and I was waiting to find out if I got the job when somebody sent me an email. "Just wondering if you're still interested in Slurpy?" the note said. I was thinking, "who are you and who is Slurpy?" And then I noticed that the note went on to say that I had done a PartyLite show at this person's house a couple of years earlier.

"You said you would take Slurpy if I were ever looking for a new home for her. Still interested?"

I absolutely was still interested!

"How much do you want for her," I asked.

"She's free — you just have to pick her up," the lady said.

While all this was going on I was looking at houses on the QT. My real estate agent said, "I think I found a place for you. It's the upstairs of a two storey house and it has a beautiful view."

"Can I bring a dog?" I asked.

Two days before Christmas Eve I learned I got the job. I picked the dog up, and took the rental house. As it turned out, by-laws stipulated that it was illegal to rent out the basement so the landlord gave me access to that as well, for the same rent as I was already committed to paying. Life unfolded quickly and smoothly. I was in flow. Things flow when you're open.

143

The Energy of Thought

And, by the way, you can't hold two energies at the same time: you can't focus on what's joyful if you're focusing on what you think is perceptively wrong. If you're telling a friend what a shitty day you've had, then you're attracting more shitty day into it. But if you talk about and live the good stuff, then you're going to attract more of the good stuff.

Thoughts are things. Powerful things. When you have positive thoughts about something, you're manifesting the development of positive outcomes. When you have negative thoughts, meh, just observe your actions and move on. You can also come up with a word to remove the negative thoughts you may have put out towards something or someone. The word I use is "delete." It sounds strange, I know, but it mitigates the energy... we *are* human. If it's all happening *for* you, not *to* you, how could your world be anything but perfect?

Sometimes we start feeling uncomfortable about a situation, and when that happens, it's tempting to go back and second-guess ourselves. That's our ego sniping at us and creating a judgement in our minds that will keep us perceptively safe. Sometimes it serves to have an uncomfortable conversation with someone, regardless of what our ego has to say on the subject. That tends to be a great way to move a lot of stuff. And having a conversation with someone without attacking them results in greater clarity and more options for enjoyment going forward. Maintaining this outlook is largely a question of perspective and if you've heard those comparisons of "glass half empty" people and "glass half full" people you'll know what I mean. Oh, and FYI – the glass is refillable!

144

FREEDOM TIP #48:

We all signed up for our own unique journey to awakening. When you truly get out of your ego those awakening-related conversations are beyond delicious! They are flowing forward into the unknown with grace and ease. Your ego will still pop up, however you will begin to see it and thank it, bless and release it, and then do whatever your ego is flipping shit about anyway.

Dancing With What Presents

Much as I'm a big believer in "Saying Yes," I recognize that just because something presents doesn't mean you have to dance with it right now. Sometimes you have to see it, feel it and determine if it's presenting in order for you to consider something about your life you hadn't considered before. It doesn't necessarily mean the opportunity is there for you to take advantage of right now. And since the Universe has your back, there's no "wrong answer" in any of this. If you say yes, and it's a no for now, it'll fall apart quickly and a redirect will appear. If it is a "yes" and we say "no" it'll keep presenting. We have this illusion of being right or being wrong because somewhere along the way humanity has been taught that there *is* a right and there *is* a wrong.

At the end of day we're all on this delicious journey – some people are going to be fat, skinny, drug addicts, smart… but that's what they came here to be in this place of humanity, this energy, this illusion of density. That's what they came to experience, so let them have their journey. Don't carry them. They're not broken and they don't need to be fixed. Their life is theirs to spend as they see fit. Perspective is in the eye of the beholder, so release yourself from the pain you carry for others.

Here's a poem by an American high school student that's a beautiful example of what I'm talking about:

From an 11th grader in Brooklyn, New York.

"Worst Day Ever?"

By Chanie Gorkin

Today was the absolute worst day ever

And don't try to convince me that there's something good in every day

Because, when you take a closer look, This world is a pretty evil place.

 Even if some goodness does shine through once in a while satisfaction and happiness don't last.

And it's not true that it's all in the mind and heart.

True happiness can be obtained

Only if one's surroundings are good

 It's not true that good exists

I'm sure you can agree that

 The reality

Creates
My attitude

 It's all beyond my control

 And you'll never in a million years hear me say that

Today was a good day

**Now read from the bottom to top.

 It's flow. It's all God. Just say "yes." Whatever it is, say some form of "yes."

Chapter Thirteen: Death

I think each soul has its own particular qualities, and when you've been really close to someone, you recognize their soul, no matter what form it takes.

- Annie Kagan

I mentioned earlier that when I got the news that my dog, Wrigley, might have a brain tumour I was devastated, and I struggled to make peace with the idea of him not being here in Earthly form any more. If you've ever lost a loved one, you know the gut-wrenching grief that goes along with the transition to a life without them. And I know it might sound disrespectful to compare the grief of losing a dog with the grief of losing a person you love, but I've known people who have experienced both and who say that there are certainly similarities.

I awoke early one morning during the months we thought we were losing Wrigley. I was about to roll over, when I felt someone sit on the edge of my bed. When I went to look, I heard a voice in my head telling me not to... so I lay there as the pain in my chest got bigger and bigger until I could no longer hold it. I had to let it go and I was told to receive. The most beautiful white light appeared in my room to assist me, upgrading and activating my heart to capacitate more love.

When I took Wrigley for a walk that day, we went to a watering hole on a nearby ranch. This watering hole is pretty small, maybe 50 x 150 feet, and it has a dock you can walk out on. It's one of Wrigley's favourite places to go.

When we approached the water, we could hear "peeew, peeew, splash." It was the sound of frogs, who seemed to be everywhere, jumping in to the water off the shore. I had never seen this kind of frog before, so I took some pictures. As I stood on the dock taking pictures of these frogs floating in the water, Wrigley plodded into the water and swam out to one of the frogs. He nose-butted it, and they sat there looking at each other for a while, both very peaceful and happy. I got a vision of a vortex that had opened up and it was shared with me that these frogs were Wrigley's Pleiadean comrades. I know that some people will consider that a pretty wild way to talk, so if I shake your tree a little, may I invite you to run with it?

People who know me well understand I have a whole other dimensional side to me — actually, you do, too — and I lean in to that aspect of who I am to receive insight and understanding I'd otherwise be unable to access. At the time, I still struggled with not being able to assist Wrigley on this journey and that day I came to peace with the fact that everything was exactly how he'd like it to be. I saw visions of amazing memories from the numerous lifetimes we've been together and there was so much love it's impossible to describe how I felt.

And I remembered that it's true: we never actually die. It's tough to believe that; trust me, I get it. We have been programmed to believe that this is it. One birth, one life, one death, and then one long run of "not being" on the planet. We have been embedded with fear of death and many of us operate from the cultural belief that if we can't see something, it can't be true. You can't see gravity, though, and it exists. Just sayin'. Even though I know this, I struggled with Wrigley's experience of this illness for a long time.

148

It was difficult for me to understand what was going on and to get that we all exist as part of a much bigger picture, beyond what we can see in this dimension. I have had many pets in my life and I've worked with all kinds of wild animals, but I have never had a connection like I do with Wrigley.

People would always say "Oh man, he is so smart and well-behaved!" How do you tell people that, well, yes he is, and he and I speak the same language?! He is actually a master that chose to come in to this dog body to be able to assist me. We were close as could be. And then suddenly one day, there he was, this dog who is everything to me sliding his back legs against the cabinet while his head dropped towards the floor. His front feet were clawing at the floor beneath him, and he had a look in his eyes that said, "the lights are on but nobody is home." I went to his side and eased his head onto my lap. I saw a vision of how his brain was firing but his body wasn't receiving as it usually would. He was having a seizure; I was shown a small tumor on his brain.

After about 15 minutes he slowly came back to his body. I called the vet and they took him in right away. They took blood to rule out any organ failures, which I knew would be negative; I had energetically scanned his entire body myself. Everything was good except for that little tumor in his head, (I always thought for some reason that a brain tumor would be bigger). I kept telling myself maybe I was wrong this time. I waited by the phone the next day and the vet called and let me know that everything was normal. So now what?

When not seizuring, Wrigley was quite happy and just wanting to continue to experience JOY in every moment possible.

As you know, Wrigley really loves to go up the mountain, so we explored more trails, and even made some of our own. I hugged him and loved him, and I cried and cried. In the moments when I thought my heart was going to break, I realised that this experience had also triggered my heart to open wide, and it allowed for so many things to come up and go. It is those things, those thick, very difficult dense things, that hurt my heart. When they come up to leave, and I resist, it actually hurts my heart.

When I allowed myself to cry, the pain subsided. I was not only crying for the shift occurring in and with my beloved best friend, I was crying for all of the things I had stuffed down into my heart, all the things I would not allow myself to experience, thinking with that pea brain again, that if I just ignored it, if I just carried on, it would not affect who I am. Eventually I realized that part of what I had to release was any energy around needing Wrigley to be there for me in a physical body. And I did.

Wrigley is still here with us today. All is well with my buddy and we're still hiking the mountain trails of Canada's West Coast. And, while it might be true that our time together on this part of this journey is measurable, the joy we give each other is not.

Sometimes we have to see the blessing in everything, including the prospective death of a loved one, hard and painful and traumatic as that might perceptively seem to be. When someone you love transitions, you have the ability to maintain an energetic connection with them—beyond the density, the crap, and the ego. That doesn't mean that you don't have periods of intense pain around missing the comfort of that person's physical presence. But you certainly can stay connected.

When someone passes, especially if their leaving was unexpected, it triggers a lot of fear and compassion. People begin to "dress rehearse" for their own tragedy, a tragedy that doesn't even exist. We are powerful creators. What if it's true that when you dress rehearse for your own death you are holding the vibration for it to manifest? What if having sad compassion for someone whose life has taken a tragic turn actually holds them in frequency of the tragedy? What if you are anchoring them in pain and suffering?

As a creator, what if you could release yourself from the story that isn't even yours and simply send those people peace and love? What would happen if everyone who was shaken could take a breath and see it is not their story? If they could step out of it and go to a place of gratitude for all that they have, and send those people peace and love? What would happen for those people?

What if you could allow them their journey without judgement of what you think it should look like? What if you could picture them in love, vitality and wellbeing?

And, finally, what if death happens for a reason? I know this sounds a bit harsh or maybe even cold. We all experience perceptive tragedy in our lives, some people perceptively more than others. What if we didn't have to perceive it as a tragedy?

When people exit their body and transition to another dimension, sometimes they get stuck in this dimension. If that happens, the spirit can linger until they have completion with something or someone. We commonly label that presence a "ghost," and a lot of people are scared of them. It's been my experience that most "ghosts" aren't evil – often the dominant emotion I pick up from them is sadness or confusion.

151

There's also ignorance of the fact they're no longer in a physical body. Now that I've had a lot more experience with these things I know how to help them move on in their journey and leave the place where they've taken up residence. There are many other people who are engaged in that work as well. Death is not something to fear. It's just another station along the journey.

FREEDOM TIP #49:

Grief can keep you from hearing the whispers of your loved one. When you are ready, you will sense them, smell them, and possibly hear them. They may leave signs in ways that will have you remember them. Know that in those moments they are with you, lovingly reminding you that they are not gone.

My Vision of Uncle Terry's Transition

Not wanting to die is very different from wanting to live. I have had many moments in my life that stopped me in my tracks and one of them was the vision I had one day that my Uncle Terry was going to die.

At the time, he was very healthy and happy. He would come and visit, and hang out with my kids and me, and on one of those visits, maybe a month after I had the vision of his death, we took the dogs for a walk. I took Uncle Terry into the woods up the side of a mountain; it had the most amazing trees and such beautiful bushes.

My uncle stopped in awe of the forest around him, and we just breathed it all in. When we got back to my place, Uncle Terry didn't look so good — he was a bit grey. He said he wasn't feeling well.

I asked him about it and the upshot was that I told him he should probably go and get himself checked out.

Within a few days, I received a call from a friend of Uncle Terry's who said that he had been so worried about Uncle Terry that he had just taken him to the hospital emergency ward.

My husband and I went straight to the hospital and found Uncle Terry there on a gurney in a hallway. He told us they had just told him that he had pancreatic cancer. He was in total shock.... I was in shock, too. We spoke to a doctor and found out that the prognosis was terrible. He was on his way out.

Somehow, I had been told. Somehow, someone had found a way to get a message to me about Uncle Terry's impending death. How was this possible? It was sad beyond measure to think of how I was going to manage without Uncle Terry in my life. Even though I knew his energy would still be available to me, no matter what, I recognized that our time together was going to change dramatically. Indeed, just a few hours after Uncle Terry died, his essence visited me while I was in the kitchen standing at the fridge. "I'm OK," he told me. "Now come on, don't be crying — I love you."

Grandpa Tommy Passes

Uncle Terry's death was not my first. In fact, death is one of those issues that keeps repeating in our lives.

Sometime before my sixth birthday I remember going to the hospital to see my Grandpa Tommy. It smelled funny in there, and there were lots of beeping sounds. I climbed up on my Grandpa Tommy's bed with him, and played with the little stuffed toy he had, a brown wiener dog with a green Peter Pan-style hat on its head.

I would sit and watch all the interesting people hustling and bustling around. Some just hung out around my Grandpa's bed, almost like they were waiting for him to do something. When it was time to go, I hopped off the bed and my dad put his hand out. I took his hand in mine and asked "Why are all those people around Grandpa Tommy's bed? Why does he look yellow?" Without a glance my dad answered that Grandpa Tommy wasn't feeling well and the people were helping him get better. Hmm, interesting.

A few days later my dad put me in the car and said he was going to the hospital to see Grandpa Tommy. He said I couldn't come this time and that he was going to drop me off at the park by the hospital for a few minutes. Those were the days when parents had no compunction about dropping their five-year-old kids off alone in a park for a few hours. We didn't wear seatbelts, either. And home alone? That wasn't just a movie back then! My dad dropped me off at the swings and said he would be back soon.

I remember playing in the park on the swings and watching the birds and the breeze on the tree branches. It was very peaceful, even with all the kids running around. I have no idea how long I was at the park, time had no meaning to me then, but eventually I could see my dad walking towards me. When he got close I could see he had tears in his eyes. He scooped me up and gave me a big hug, and then he handed me the stuffed dog that had been on Grandpa Tommy's bed. "Grandpa Tommy wanted you to have this," he said. "He died today." Now, I really didn't understand what this meant. I was told that Grandpa Tommy had gone to be with God in heaven, and some well-wishers told me that I would never see him again.

154

They held Grandpa Tommy's funeral on my sixth birthday. There were a lot of sad people. Many years have gone by since then, and still to this day my Grandpa Tommy sits and observes my family. He never interferes, he simply observes.

We Cry For What We Think We Have Lost

We humans have so many rituals around death, so many fears. One of the chief expectations many people have is that as soon as we die, we go to spend time with God. A client asked me recently what God means to me. To me God is everything. It's you, it's me, and it's the grass, the trees, the birds and the bees. It is all of it. I love the true meaning of the saying "Namaste." It's a short form for the saying, "I honour the place in you in which the entire Universe dwells. I honour the place in you which is of Love, Truth Light and Peace. When you are in that place in you, and I am in that place in me, we are one."

Namaste. This struck a chord with me and resonated at a very young age. It made sense. However, since starting this journey of awakening I also take from it the understanding that we are not one.....we are of the one. We are all here with our own little piece of the puzzle. We each bring our gifts for this awakening journey and we are all of the one.

Likewise, we never really die.

This came home for me when my great-grandmother, my father's grandmother, was ill. Ma Mère, we called her, French for "My Mother." She had been in the hospital for a while and when I had last seen her in the hospital, she was not doing well.

155

Nobody expected her to live much longer, but she had spoken to me for a while in French. I had no idea what she was saying and my Grandpa hushed her.

I remember looking into her beautiful eyes, which were so wise, and so full of love; they were a comfortable place to gaze.

We used to visit my Ma Mère a lot before she became ill, and I loved going to see her. She was very kind, and smart and she had the most beautiful eyes. My dad's energy would soften and relax, unfolding like flowers opening up for the sun, when we visited her.

She was a tiny little French woman who spoke perfect English with no accent. I remember her saying once that "if the French speak English with a French accent, they are lazy!"

We had a gentle visit with Ma Mère at the hospital and then went home.

A few nights later, I was awakened from my sleep to see Ma Mère standing at the end of my bed in a long white gown. She looked peaceful.

I said her name and she just smiled, and then I got a bit freaked out as I realized that this was impossible, or so I had been told.

In the morning, I told my mom what had happened and, sure enough, Ma Mère had passed away during the night.

My mom was a bit surprised at what I told her, but she didn't make a big deal about it.

The shell Ma Mère had been walking around in might have broken down, but her spirit was alive and well.

Now when someone transitions, I'm quite accustomed to a peaceful visit from their spirit. It's nothing to fear or dread. A death is no ending, and we don't have to cry for the person who left. Actually, they didn't really leave. They're still here, still around, still visiting and still watching over us with love.

Here's the thing to remember about death: from the moment we are born into this physical body on the planet, we have perceptively begun our journey towards death. Is this the life when we are called to step into the truth of who we truly are?

What is it about your journey that brings up fear? How can you see the truth of who you are? It is time to wake up!

Regardless of when we transition from our physical body, we are called to full circle all of those uncomfortable things that come up for us on our journey.

We can be in total wellness and vitality regardless of our physical state. We get to choose Love or Fear! You are so loved! You matter! You are more than enough!

FREEDOM TIP #50:

Get yourself into a peaceful space, take a few deep belly breaths pulling in packets of white sparkling light, and ask to be shown a sign, or to have a visit in a dream state. When we are sleeping, it is much easier for our higher levels to show us things. When you're ready they will come to you.

Chapter Fourteen: Playing with Energy

There is a voice that doesn't use words. LISTEN.

I closed my mouth and spoke to you in a hundred million ways.

- Rumi

Somewhere along the way we've all been taught that there's right and there's wrong. But at the end of day, we're all on this delicious journey together. Some people are going to be brilliant scientists, some are going to be high school drop outs. Some will have physical challenges, others will be excellent athletes. Some of us turn out to be drug addicts, and others become company CEOs.

I believe that whatever we choose to be in this life is what we decided we were going to be before we arrived. If someone is struggling with an issue, then it seems to me that that is what they decided they wanted to explore. That's what they signed up for in this place of humanity, this energy, this illusion of density. That's what they came here to experience and to full circle. So, let them have their journey – they're not broken and they don't need to be fixed. Everything is all up to them.

I also believe that there is an energetic component to our lives and as I explored in the previous chapter, death is not an "ending" just as birth is not a "beginning." Our spirits are eternal and untethered.

Astro Travel? Really?

Throughout my life I've experienced many different things that seem very strange to a lot of other people. When I was little I can remember putting myself into a very relaxed state and then feeling a sensation like I was leaving my body. It took me a long time to master moving around in this state, but I did, going on little "trips" around the house without the benefit of my body.

In the beginning, I would bang up against walls and doors; I felt as if I were a balloon filled with helium trying to maneuver around the house. It was hilarious! After practising for a while I figured out that all I had to do was *intend* a location, and I would end up there. OK, it sounds perceptively crazy, but you can move through walls in that state — there actually are no human limitations. I would float around the house from room to room, *intending* my way through the house.

I remember watching my mom and my sister having a conversation in the living room on the other side of the house and wondering if they could see me. Nope, pretty sure they couldn't.

When I was done travelling, I'd come slamming back into my body. It was like a crash landing and it was very jarring: I was a very big being of energy attempting to fit back into my physical body.

Astro traveling is a fancy word for having an out-of-body experience. You leave your body behind and this is something that anyone can do. Everyone astro-travels but some people are more aware of it than others. Have you ever had one of those dreams where you are falling and then you wake up just before you hit the ground?

160

You know that jolting feeling that goes along with it? That's a crash landing after traveling. Or maybe you have had a dream that you are falling. Or flying. Or have you done a guided meditation? You can see, feel, hear and experience things this way, and it feels like you were really there.

We travel to many different dimensions, whether we are aware of it or not. We visit other aspects of ourselves in other lifetimes, to assist us here and there.

I was very aware I was doing this when I was younger, and it was fun for me. While I learned to master the art of traveling without my physical body, I would listen in on conversations and visit people.

I couldn't always hear the conversations and I believe I was only shown what was in the highest for me to see and hear. If people don't want you to see or hear things, you won't.

The point is, though, that you are not your body. It is a vehicle for taking you places but you don't have to be limited to the places your body can physically go.

You can climb out of your body, at least the energetic component of who you are can, and experience the Universe another way.

FREEDOM TIP #51:

The great thing I learned is that you are always connected to your body and it is your choice to leave or stay, or to invite others in. You have this energetic cord that keeps you connected to your body.

Animals and Energy

Another component of energy is that we are able to communicate energetically with each other and, more particularly, with animals. That's a huge part of who I am: I'm passionate about animal communication and, like many of the other people who have developed their capability to do that, I take the integrity of the process very seriously.

Communicating with animals is like tapping into the energy flowing within them and from them and picking up on the thought patterns and emotional patterns that they are emanating.

When I communicate with animals I'm also tapping into the people who think they "own" the animals and it always amazes me how we get the animals we need, not necessarily the ones we want.

I used to train animals for the movie industry and I had a lot of amazing conversations with the animals I worked with in those years. One day I saw a woman struggling with a dog who was just not listening to her. I asked her if I could help her out and she gratefully said, "Yes!" I took her dog, had a little conversation with him and said "that's enough -- I'm the leader here and you're going to follow." The dog told me that he felt that he had to be on guard and protect his person all the time. I told the lady that she should stand in her power more, and be the leader this dog wanted her to be.

"Put your shoulders back and stand in that power," I said. "This issue is really about you – this dog needs to feel that it doesn't have to be on duty all the time." Just that fast, things changed for this lady.

162

Once when I was working in the film industry I was responsible for a cougar who was being filmed for part of a documentary. His name was Jake. I just loved Jake, and he loved me right back.

While we were working on the documentary, I had Jake on a thick chain, although I had no fear of this big cat. As part of the shoot the producers asked me to take Jake through the bush. I had a walkie talkie with me and I had a meat pouch around my waist as part of my training gear.

And all of a sudden I realized, "Hey, I'm walking through the bush with raw meat basically wrapped around my belly and a cat that's bigger and more powerful than I am who is on the end of a chain that I can pull but I cannot push. Okay, Houston, let's hope everything goes smoothly!"

I could hear the guys on the walkie-talkies chattering back and forth a lot and Jake started to look around a lot. He was looking anxiously up at me, and I said, "You're OK buddy." His body language shifted and he started to posture. One of the guys on the radio announced that he found fresh cougar scat, and fresh tracks, which meant there was a wild cougar in the area at that very moment.

Jake's eyes turned a deeper shade of green, his ears went flat and he looked really scared. The film crew was 60 feet away behind the tree line at the bottom of a steep hill, ready to take the shot, and I looked at Jake and started to talk to him.

"We're totally safe, that other cougar is not coming anywhere near us, there's nothing to worry about," I repeated. It took me about 30 minutes of baby-talking him into feeling safe, letting him know what to expect, before he started to relax.

163

He was saying things to me like, "I don't want to do this anymore, I just want out." "We're going to go down to your crate," I said. "Don't worry."

I yelled out to the crew that the cougar was done for the day, we had to stop and everybody had to get out of there immediately.

"We just need this one last shot and we're done," the producer said.

"You don't get it," I said. "This cougar is done – you cannot negotiate a better trailer, or a nicer meal and convince him to stay focused. He's a wild animal and he's going to flip his shit if he doesn't get some down time right now!"

Everybody was quite upset, and I knew this was going to cost the producers a lot of money. But I just kept talking to Jake and reassuring him that everything was going to be OK. "I'm going to put you in your crate and you'll be safe," I said.

Once Jake was in his crate I was able to unwind. I sat on the ground beside him and I told him he did great. But really, he'd been assisting *me* in standing in who I am.

Anybody can communicate with animals, of course. If you're not understanding your dog or cat or whatever, don't get frustrated. Send pictures to them energetically and they will send you pictures back. That's where you start.

People sometimes ask me how I can communicate freely with animals and still count myself a meat eater. That's a good question. I know a number of people who are vegan and often their biggest rationale for their lifestyle is that they don't want any animals to come to harm on their account.

My belief is that all animals have agreed to come in to being at this time on the planet in order to assist humanity in our evolution. Some of them are our companions, and some provide entertainment. Some provide wool for clothing and others provide food for our physical support. We all signed up for all kinds of experiences and some of the less attractive roles by animals serve to wake up humanity.

When I eat, I bless everything and go into a long wormhole of appreciation for the animal, the plants and all the ingredients that have served me by providing food for my family.

I also express gratitude to all of the people in the food supply chain who had to work towards ensuring we had safe and healthy food to eat.

We all have a purpose and it's constantly changing, it's a journey. We each have to own our own journey. A lot of people don't want to own their journey – there's a lot of shitty stuff that's gone on in life for people. You are not that story, that is not who you are, but all those things on your journey have brought you to where you are now. You are a survivor. More than that, you are a "thriver." Own it!

FREEDOM TIP #52:

Place your hands over your food before you eat and simply go into gratitude for everything you are about to receive. Some of you may see visions or sense the connection. When you eat your food, slow down and enjoy it. Smell it, and hold it in your mouth for two minutes before you chew. Feel the food. Taste all of it. Expand the love and appreciation out.

Grounding Your Energy

If you're having a shitty day, have the best shitty day ever. You know the scenario: you're running late and you can't find your shoes or your keys or your lunch bag. Maybe your hair dryer broke or the furnace stopped working or the freezer shut down.

On top of that the kids are in crisis, you have a disagreement with a family member and your boss is unhappy about something you forgot to do yesterday.

The car won't start, traffic is bad and the weather is ferocious. It all just sucks. So immerse yourself in it. And know that everything is happening *for* you. Running late might be the Universe's way of keeping you from an accident. Conflict with people gives you an opportunity to look at how you are showing up in your life. It's all happening *for* you, not at all *"to"* you. When you release the resistance to the day, and embrace what is arriving, you shift the energy. Surrender. Or....

If you want to shake that shitty day, go to the park or the forest or somewhere that Nature resides. You cannot be angry in the forest, it's impossible. The forest is like a washing machine for human beings: you've got all these energies charging through you and the fresh air will sweep through them and you, and rinse your insides clean as a whistle.

FREEDOM TIP #53:

Want to know what frequency you are vibrating out? Look at what is showing up in your life. You are a powerful creator: you get to choose what you want.

I first had this feeling in action when I was just a little girl. I was excited one day when my parents told me and my sister that we would be moving to a small town just over an hour away. I was excited and nervous. It was going to be great! We moved to the most beautiful country home imaginable. It was a ranch style house with a big beautiful yard that backed onto the most magical forest I had ever seen. The roads were gravel and the neighbours were so far away you couldn't see them from our house. A feeling of peace came over me when I was out in the forest. It was unlike anything I had ever experienced before. I belonged there. My dogs and I explored endlessly in trees that seemed to go on forever. There was a beautiful creek winding through what I called the monkey trees. These were trees that bent over from the root and touched the ground. They were incredibly strong, just like monkey bars. The sounds of the birds and squirrels relaxed me into a blissful calm. This was my heaven on Earth and any time I was in turmoil, I would walk in the forest and ground myself in the beautiful energy of nature. It's something I still do today. And it is still magical.

There are other ways of grounding yourself. For example:

FREEDOM TIP #54:

Imagine roots growing out through the souls of your feet. They go down through the floor, through the concrete, and all the way deep down through all the beautiful layers of the Earth's crust, deep, deep down until you see an amazing metallic ball. Your roots wrap around this ball, and stay connected to you like an umbilical cord to Mother Earth, moving freely and easily with you throughout the day.

How Energy Works

My husband had been working in a small town in Alberta and I was planning to visit him. I've been a traveller most of my life, the traveling gypsy in me having been awoken when I was about 12. So I am no stranger to packing and preparing to depart. The day before my visit, I was unloading the dishwasher in the kitchen when I had a vision of an airplane going down in the Rockies near where we live; I saw myself opening the emergency exit.

I was stunned at what I was shown and I rejected the vision, if that's at all possible. Some people I know are accustomed to getting messages like this from their subconscious mind/Universe. Others find the concept a bit fishy. Wherever you are on that continuum, you're right. We're all right. This just happens to be a part of how I navigate my world. I carried on with my day and even changed the battery in my alarm clock to be sure I'd be up in time for my flight. (Although, truth to tell, I haven't used an alarm clock to wake me up in years).

The next morning, I awoke before the alarm and said: "Something amazing is going to happen today! I wonder what it is?" Just like usual. I fed the dogs, said good bye to my girls and headed out to the car with my bags. I was off! It was interesting to note that, although I love to travel, I was feeling very anxious as I drove towards the airport. I kept seeing a vision of an airplane going down. I wasn't enjoying the feelings I was experiencing. As I was getting close to the airport I looked in my rear view mirror and saw a police car zipping up behind me with the lights flashing. I pulled over, thinking I must have been speeding, but nope, he just kept on going.

168

The next thing I knew I was seeing a vision of a plane down in the middle of the road with emergency vehicles all around it. I stayed parked at the side of the road and took a deep breath, relaxed my body and simply asked my higher levels to tell me what this was all about? I was told to just carry on, that everything was being looked after. I pulled back out onto the road, and trusted that things would be great. Still feeling a bit uneasy, I headed off to the airport.

When I arrived at security with my boarding pass ready to go, I stopped and asked an employee if I was required to do anything else before going through to my gate. She looked at my ticket and informed me that my flight had been cancelled. I was freaking elated! I was smiling and then asked her the reason for the cancellation.

She said that there were some mechanical issues and she printed off a new ticket for a later flight that afternoon. Well, I was as happy as a pig in a mud bath. I called my husband and told him to go back to the job site, that I wouldn't be arriving until later. His ego was not impressed, however when I told him my story, he was just great. It turned out that he was needed on the job site that day and it all worked out.

It was interesting looking at all of this unknown landscape. The Universe has your back and, in fact, it has a much bigger plan than what we could ever understand because there is so much going on all at the same time. I left the airport and went to find a cup of tea. My body was adjusting to the release of the anxiety.

When I was driving home I decided to listen to my phone messages. There was a call from a woman who had looked me up on the Internet.

169

"Hi!" she said. "I'm in town here for the day and I found you on the Internet. I know it's short notice but I'd like to come in for a session with you today." I laughed out loud in my car. I called her back and said: "Wow you are a powerful creator!" I explained I had no clients as I was supposed to be on a plane to Calgary but it was cancelled. She came for a session and it was magical.

What if you could experience anxiety and then simply calm yourself and feel that the Universe has your back always, regardless of the choices you make with a brain that is so much smaller than can accommodate the thoughts of the Universe?

What if logic slowed down your process?

How does your life look and feel when you live in flow?

FREEDOM TIP #55:

When you are struggling, you are in ego; when it is all coming together with grace and ease, you are in flow.

Another Aspect of Energy

I had some interesting experiences as a young person and I can remember one especially interesting time took place on an evening when my parents had invited some friends over. They'd enjoyed a few beverages and decided to do an experiment. They placed a glass cup upside down on the coffee table. Then they stuck a pin into the middle of a cork from a wine bottle. Next, they took a piece of paper about the size of a sticky note, and folded it corner to corner, then corner to corner the other way so it had a point and four triangular sections.

They then balanced the paper with the point up on the pin in the cork so it would spin if you blew on it.

Each adult took a turn at trying to use their mind to move the paper. Everyone would watch to make sure no one was blowing on it.

Everyone had a little bit of success with this project and I was very fascinated to watch it all. They asked me if I wanted a turn and I said, yes, I sure did! This looked like fun.

I closed my eyes and watched the paper spin in my mind's eye. While my eyes were closed, I could hear a couple of the adults "oooh" and "ahhh." And I opened my eyes to see the paper doing exactly what I had seen it do in my mind's eye. It was spinning *fast*. What a trip!

The Darker Side

"God has the final word on everything: even the devil obeys God."

- Kaayla Vedder

This life therefore is not righteousness, but growth in righteousness, not health, but healing, not being but becoming, not rest but exercise. We are not yet what we shall be, but we are growing toward it, the process is not yet finished, but it is going on, this is not the end, but it is the road. All does not yet gleam in glory, but all is being purified."

- Martin Luther

Not all aspects of energy are as entertaining as parlour tricks on a Sunday afternoon. I've had perceptively negative experiences with energy, as well. When I was about 15 years old I had some trouble sleeping, and it was such a big problem that my parents eventually took me to the doctor. I thought "Ahh there's an explanation for these strange sensations I've been having, and we'll get this all nicely figured out now."

The doctor said I was experiencing a drop into deep Rapid Eye Movement (REM) sleep for my body that left my mind behind. I was still alert. In other words, it's a state where you can't move but you're awake and aware of everything around you. This was a great scientific explanation but the prescription for sleeping pills he gave me didn't address the feeling of something trying to come into my body. I had a knowing that the sleeping pills would not assist the situation.

Even after visiting the doctor, I would find myself awake in bed at night and unable to move any part of my body. I would lie in bed and have what felt like an energetic battle with something. I could feel it trying to get into my body. One night, when I was lying on my back unable to move, I could feel the comforter starting to move. I could feel it coming up around my neck and getting tighter, and while this was happening, I began to pray. Now, I was not brought up with any kind of religion, however I was able to connect with Source, and the blanket released. I was able to get up and out of bed. I was afraid to sleep. I had not shared any of this with anyone; I truly thought something was terribly wrong with me. I remember calling all kinds of churches and explaining what was happening; the most common response was that I was being possessed and required an exorcism.

"What the…? How does this even happen? What the heck is an exorcism?" I continued to have this battle every night until finally I was no longer afraid. I was annoyed by the inconvenience of this whole situation, and I was exhausted. I went to bed and the same thing started to happen again. All I could ever do was rub my teeth together, back and forth. This was the only part of me that would move. I would try and call out to my mom but I still couldn't move.

I kept on praying and then started saying, "You do not have permission to be here, this is my body, now *get out*! I began to see, in my mind's eye, my entire body filling with light, and the struggle became very intense.

Words came blasting out of my mouth in a voice I still to this day could not replicate. "Holy Shit!" I thought. Then I was up and out my bedroom door. I was sobbing, I went to my mom and told her I needed help, "I think I am crazy, you have to call someone and get me into Riverview (a mental hospital)."

Luckily for me, my mom was open to these shifts of energy, although she had just started on her path of consciously awakening. She had been told by someone a long time ago that one of her girls was a gifted healer and that she would require some assistance on her path. Oh my God, I was so relieved! My mom called a woman to come and assist me in getting whatever or whoever it was out of my room.

The next day, a tiny petite woman named Heather arrived. She had dark shoulder-length hair, beautiful brown eyes and she weighed maybe 80 pounds soaking wet. Her very tall and gruff-looking husband came with her. Both of them had a beautiful, calming energy all around them and it was peaceful to be in their presence.

173

We all went into my room, turned the lights down and lit some candles. Heather was sitting in a rocking chair facing my bed; I was sitting on the edge of my bed with Heather's husband beside me.

The next thing you know, that same voice that had come blasting out of my mouth the previous night was now coming out of her mouth. It was a male voice that claimed to belong to a biker who had died unexpectedly; he saw my light and followed me home. He said "I was just trying to have a little fun" and he wasn't buying that he had passed over...I remember thinking how messed up this was.

Heather's husband asked if I wanted to say anything to this entity and all I could say was "You need to leave. You are not welcome here." Heather and her husband left our property and took this entity with them. I was able to see one of Heather's guides, a large native man dressed in skins with long dark hair in two braids. He helped escort this entity off our property and eventually assisted him to cross over.

I wasn't sure how I felt about all of this. I was relieved to hear that I wasn't crazy, and it was nice to meet someone who understood what I had always seen, felt and experienced in so many ways. I was no longer "the sensitive one."

I was truly able to share with someone all of the many perceptively bizarre experiences I had hidden from my family and friends. I don't share this in order to freak anyone out, although I must say that I was really freaked out at the time. What I learned from this experience was how powerful prayer and intention are, especially when you combine them with your own determination to stand in your own light.

FREEDOM TIP #56:

When you let go of your fear and stand in your light nothing — and I mean *nothing* — can touch you. Be the observer.

Bizarre Telephone Messages

I would grow accustomed to these strange experiences as time went on. Sometime before my "biker experience," I was home alone. Well, not really "alone," as I had my beautiful best friends with me: Dusty who was a large white German Shepherd with black fur around his eyes like a bandit, and my little ginger Brandy, a mixed breed of Irish setter and cocker spaniel. Brandy had a long tail and beautiful red hair on a tiny head with small ears that flopped down softly. She was a precious Heinz 57 kind of doggie.

My parents were early adopters on the cordless phone front and the base for the phone was in their bedroom. The base for the phone had a call button on it that lit up a red light when you pushed it, and it made the handset beep so you could easily find it. One night, I was home alone and sitting in the family room, which was on the complete opposite side of the house from my parent's bedroom. Much to my surprise, the cordless phone handset started beeping. I got up from the sofa and went through the kitchen to the living room. It was very dark in there, thanks in part to the big floor-to-ceiling windows that took up two of the four walls. As I got closer to my parents' room, my dog Dusty started to growl. It was a low growl at first but as I got closer to my parents' room, he began to growl louder.

At the time, I was thinking that this was because of the loud beeping that was still coming from both the phone and the base. We entered my parents' room. To my right was their big king-sized bed and to my left was a large dresser. At the end of the bed there was a window with a sliding glass door, again it ran from floor to ceiling along the entire wall. In one corner of the room sat my dad's tall dresser, and on it sat the telephone base. I could see from where I was standing that the red light was going on and off with the beeping of the phone. As I got a bit closer, Dusty started to bark like crazy. His hackles went up and I could see that the button was being physically pushed down and then released, — repeatedly.

I was officially freaked out! I ran out of the bedroom and went straight to the kitchen. I pulled the battery out of the cordless phone and I picked up the kitchen phone, which was connected to the wall outlet. I dialed a friend who was at work and as soon as she answered the phone I started to speak, but I could no longer hear her answer back. I was praying that she could still hear me so I kept talking, even though all I could hear was a deafening fuzzy sound on the phone. My dog was still barking and standing right beside me, his hackles still up. I was so freaked out, so full of fear, that I was crying and saying into the phone that I didn't know what was happening. I hung up the phone and tried using it again but the noise on the line was even louder than before: no dial tone, just fuzz. I tried dialing a number and I got nothing. I had nowhere to go and no way to get anywhere.

I sat down on the kitchen floor and cried in fear. My dog stood beside me growling at the air around me and then I remembered the power of the light.

I surrounded myself and concentrated on light and love filling my entire being. Then I began to fill the room with light, while praying to God and the angels to assist me. Right away I could feel the energy moving, and then, in my mind's eye, I saw the entity that had been in control of the phone: it was a dark shadowy figure, not like a person, just a blob of energy. I saw it leave.

The entire front of our house was floor-to-ceiling windows with two sliding glass doors in the middle and as I sat there, shaking, I saw headlights coming down the driveway and my friend arrived at the glass door. I was so relieved to see her! Everything had calmed down by then. My best friend now knew about the kinds of things that had been going on for me; she was still my friend.

The Journey Forward

Those were long years ago and much has happened for me since then. I've become much more comfortable with who I am and what I am on the planet to accomplish. Much of it revolves around helping people become more comfortable with who they are and how they experience their lives.

Many people come to me with perceptively strange stories, like these ones, that don't frighten them. They want to make some sense of it all.

Sometimes I organize groups to go to places where there is a lot of energy and a lot of dimensional shifting. A lot of our experiences revolve around animals – large snakes that could have been aggressive but were not, large stags that don't run when they see us, rabbits that fearlessly hold their place in front of us.

177

One of the points of the journey is to connect to Source and we do that quite often through nature. People on my groups can be authentically true to themselves and we often explore some of the other dimensions available to us on this planet... the question of stargates, off-planetary life, and so on. I came in with a lot of well-flexed muscles in a lot of areas. I don't have a lot of judgement around anyone else's beliefs or dogma. I was probably brought up in the least prejudicial home in the world – my dad was a pilot and he flew to all kinds of different countries. He'd tell us about them with a sense of fascination, rather than judgement, and my sister and I learned to accept the fact that we're all different.

But on top of it all, I have some sensitivities that not everybody expresses comfortably or even accepts as possibilities. I don't necessarily know why I'm like that, other than I think some of us send out a signal of some sort, like some kind of beacon. It's like we're here to broadcast a particular radio frequency for others to hear and we're being called as leaders to assist all humanity in recognizing that everything in life comes down to either love or fear, and that anything that comes from a place of fear is not in the highest.

Where Does Our Creator Fit In?

I believe that our Creator sees us as unlimited beings and he or she thought you were a good idea. Incongruences in the way we live are created from the judgments we and others have, and these all stem from fear. Fear of not being enough, fear of not deserving, fear of damnation, shame and more. These fears come from a time on Earth when the energy was very different.

If I can go "off road" for a moment, I believe — as many other people I know believe — that once upon a time, agreements were made between different races of light beings that lived in numerous planetary systems.

The beings that came to play here on planet Earth made agreements to come here with a mission, knowing that once they arrived here on this planet in a physical body, with all this density, they might not recall the mission or the gifts that were innately theirs to enjoy.

You don't owe anything to anyone and I don't believe in something called "Karma." That idea comes from a place of duality, fear, and a requirement to live a perceptively "good" life; again this involves more judgement.

At one time, long before the most recent energy shifts, there was a Karmic grid system in place.

This system controlled humanity by way of thought forms — dictating through fear and defining who people were in that life stream. This powerful grid is no longer in place.

Humanity woke up to the possibilities of choice and free will and began to choose new ways of being. Standing more in who they truly are, and letting go of the constraints of the karmic system.

What if there is no right or wrong? What if there are only experiences we have all chosen to have on each journey to propel us forward in the awakening of all of humanity?

What if your purpose here on Earth is to simply open your heart wide and experience things through love?

When you put energy out into the Universe the Universe reflects back that same energy.

As you learn to experience fear, doubt, unworthiness (to name a few), you go from this beautiful blissful place of experiencing divine, unconditional love, to a place that is thick with the density of fear. You learn to fear things, you accept that the information you are given by others — your parents, for example — is true.

In my own case, I learned to not share my experiences and I convinced myself early on that I was unlovable and that nobody liked me, and, voilà! I got what I expected.

I was sending out an energy of fear, fear that people would learn about the things I was experiencing, and think that I was a nutbar.

I felt I had to protect myself, keep myself safe.

But the truth is, there is no need to be "protected." We are already safe.

And while it's wonderful for us to learn from one another, we want to make sure we don't "guru-ize" anyone. There is no room for ego.

FREEDOM TIP #57:

To FLY (Fully Love Yourself), requires compassion for where you are on your journey and FYI there is no destination. When you fully love yourself — FLY — everything else just melts away.

I've created a meditation series called 'Freedom 21', which is 21 days of quick morning and evening meditations that anyone can do.

Go to: www.Kaaylavedder.com or www.freedom21.ca and check out the services and products available.

Post Script

If you want to change the world, pick up your pen and write.

- Martin Luther

I was on the last day of an awakening retreat and I happened to sit beside one of the other participants who I had not yet had a chance to spend much time with.

She was so cute and perky and we had a great conversation, during which I asked what she did. Susan Crossman said she was a writer, editor and book coach and after we had spoken for a few minutes she said, "I bet you have a book inside you."

I said that I wasn't a writer and she didn't push it. But as soon as I got home from that trip I was asked to participate in a collaborative book and I said, "Yes!"

Then my ego freaked out and I went into total overwhelm. I called Susan and left her a message and I said "Oh my God, I don't know what I'm doing!"

My daughter had a track meet and I went off to cheer her on. She was in her joy, streaming along the track like a forceful wind and I was in my joy just watching her, when Susan called me. She broke the process of writing a book down for me into little baby steps so that I couldn't possibly feel overwhelmed – it was all so logical and doable and she said, "OK, Kaayla, we're going to do this and this and this, and I've got the timeline, and it's not a big deal, we'll get there."

I let out my air and I felt so supported by the entire Universe. It *was* a big deal, because I didn't stop my life, I just put the project out to the Universe and kept going. I felt so supported.

And it *was* easy and it *was* simple. The hard part was getting over my ego. Susan kept saying to me "this is what editors are for." I'm so appreciative of her support. But that is exactly how the Universe works. When you require the help, it shows up. When you need advice, a little voice whispers in your ear. When you need an editor and book coach, her name pops up seemingly out of nowhere. It is all vast and perfect and amazing. And connecting your spirit to the timeless work of the Universe is a process that will pull you ever onward. Anxiety is about living in a future that doesn't exist yet. Stay present, connect to the Universe and know that you are completely and fully taken care of.

You Cannot Change the Past

Some people get stuck on the shoals of the past while on their journey of expansion. You cannot change the past, so there's really no benefit to wondering if you could have done something differently. It's not about what you have done or not done that matters, in fact, it's the judgements you hold about yourself and others that bind you. When you can see that this is all happening *for* you, and not *to* you, the past will no longer hold you back. Part of that process requires you to love who you are NOW; as you're more loving and patient and forgiving with yourself now, as the judgements fall away, alomg with all the pain, hurt, and feelings of unworthiness.

When you can see things from 30,000 feet above this density, with the eyes of love and compassion and gratitude, then you are connecting to Source. This is about Love.

Feel this until it makes deep sense to you. Every one of us came here to this life, at this time, to bring the gift of who we truly are.

We came in to this life forgetting who and what we truly are, however I tend to believe that we know that there is more. I believe that we know, at some deep level of our being, that we have a purpose beyond what we see, and that purpose is to bring love and light to the density and shadow that we created from our own fearful thoughts and beliefs.

We all chose to go into this perceptive darkness to be a victim, a predator, both and more, we have been all of it.

The way to raise the vibration into the Fifth Dimension of Heaven on Earth, is to be all of who we are, and love ourselves fully, lifting that part of who we are into the light. Thus can we shift all of consciousness.

You are never alone. We have legions of light beings pulsing their energies of love our way. They are our cheerleaders; they are rooting for us all.

Love who you are now in this moment, release the judgements and know that there is nothing to forgive.

Experience how it feels to be totally and completely in love yourself, with all of your perfect imperfections. See how it begins to work in your life.

If you have children, know that you can't do things that are either right or wrong for them.

They chose their own path before they came into this physical body and the best way you can support them, on whatever journey they have chosen, is to completely accept and love all of who you are.

Be the example. Understand that you are not broken and you don't need to be fixed, and nobody else does, either.

The more you love all of it, the more grace and ease that will come into your life and all of those connected to you.

Your Body is Your Guide

The Universe speaks to us in whispers, at first.

If we don't listen to the whispers, the Universe speaks a little louder. If we still ignore the messages Source is sending, eventually we get hit with a cosmic two-by-four.

Our bodies are our biggest guides in all of this. Goose bumps, a sudden fatigue, a sore knee, a racing heart. What is your body telling you?

I am here to assist people in releasing their pain by sharing tools and moving blocked energy so you can live in flow and freedom. If you feel you are ready to go on the journey into greater love and delight, I invite you to get in touch with me via www.kaaylavedder.com.

Let's dissolve the things that are keeping you from your life of dreams. And let's replace them with the energy that will bring you release from anxiety.

In the meantime, remember that Nature is the quickest way to connect with Source.

Have you noticed how Nature doesn't struggle?

When a little seed lands in a crack on the concrete, it just grows up through the concrete.

It doesn't say "this is *soooo* hard!" It just does what it is here to do.

 An apple tree doesn't struggle to produce apples. They just unfold naturally as a result of a process that the apple tree is simply following.

So, reconnecting with Nature will remind you of how simple things can be for you.

It will open your heart, reconnect you with love, help you release judgement.

Your guides and angels, who are aspects of you, are assisting you, all of you. You can trust in them because they are you. They're here to help you break the perceptively harmful rules you've been living with for years, and to help you stop trying to control every little detail of your existence.

What's more, they'll also be cheering madly for you as you take all of the steps necessary to reclaim your life.

Naked and Awake is not just the endpoint we seek as creations of a higher power. It's also an ongoing recipe for expansive living. And this I wish for you as an audience and as a companion on the journey to greater consciousness.

Love bombs,

- **Kaayla Vedder**

About the Author:

Kaayla Vedder works remotely with most of her clients and from that auspicious insight; she developed the phrase "Kripa Quantum Healing."

She is a freedom accelerator and quantum healer, who uses the Kripa technique for integrated results.

Kaayla works with people to end their suffering. These tend to be people who know there is more to life and who don't know how to get what they seek, although they have tried many avenues for relief.

She bridges people to their higher levels, guiding and assisting them to release the entanglements and beliefs of life times.

Kaayla assists in shifting the frequency people are vibrating out and removes entities that can be the cause of anxiety, stress illness, injuries and more.

She is a witness to the dance of divine grace. When she assists her clients to experience big shifts, beautiful things begin to happen. Physical bodies begin to flow as everything starts working together to generate 100% infinite potential or better. Life times of soul memory or cell memory begin to unravel, old limiting beliefs and contracts completely dissolve, and activations and downloads begin to happen as, with Kaayla's guidance, her clients remember the powerful creators they truly are.

Kaayla has been a healer for many years and in her investigation and experience of many of the world's leading healing modalities she realized that her process is unique and difficult to define.

Sitting at her computer one day, having another go at the issue of capturing in words what she does for her clients, the word "Kripa" suddenly popped into her awareness.

Never having heard of the word, she researched it and discovered that it's about being released from the karmic journey and disentangling from prior lifetimes to embrace the fullness of what is available.

Manor House
www.manor-house-publishing.com
905-648-2193

Manor House
www.manor-house-publishing.com
905-648-2193

Manor House
www.manor-house-publishing.com
905-648-2193

Manor House
www.manor-house-publishing.com
905-648-2193